Finishing Strong

A memoir.

Dee Horwitz

iUniverse, Inc.
New York Bloomington

Finishing Strong
A memoir.

iUniverse books may be ordered through booksellers or by contacting:

iUniverse
1663 Liberty Drive
Bloomington, IN 47403
www.iuniverse.com
1-800-Authors (1-800-288-4677)

Because of the dynamic nature of the Internet, any Web addresses or links contained in this book may have changed since publication and may no longer be valid.

ISBN: 9781450242837 (sc)
ISBN: 9781450242844 (ebk)

Printed in the United States of America

iUniverse rev. date: 7/26/2010

For the Olson Family,
And with love to my daughters,
Carol, Nancy and JoAnne

Contents

Author's Preface

Facts fade away. I found few hard facts and documents to tell me about the early life of Carl and Carrie Olson and their twelve children. Obituaries, my grandfather's will, and interviews provided me with the basis for my book. In *Finishing Strong*, I looked at life on the farm less than 100 years ago and traveled through eight decades, into the 21st century.

It was not my intention to make the book into a memoir. However, I soon ran out of information about the Olson family and found myself reflecting on my own life. I realized that my transformation from that innocent and trusting farmer's daughter was as amazing as the changes in our society and lifestyle over the past 80 years.

I remember the time I spent at the farm quite well. And I did research many of the stories that have been handed down from generation to generation and, when possible, examined records to verify information.

All the Olson cousins have contributed their memories. Granted, our memories can be elusive and changing, faulty or very good. Often, it doesn't matter: It's just a good story.

Sorting out the names and all the name changes that were made in our ancestry is a task I did not care to tackle. I'm a journalist, a story-teller, not a genealogist. Before surnames were required by law for tax purposes, children often were identified as the daughters (dotters) of, or the sons of the father.

The story told to me and the one I have told for years was that my paternal grandfather came to Minnesota from Sweden and thought there were too many Pedersons in the area so he changed his name from Pederson to Olson. And when my maternal grandfather emigrated to Minnesota from Norway he thought there were too many Olsons so he changed his name from Olson to Pederson. It's a great story, one that I didn't want to destroy by tracing my ancestry.

However, now I know that it is at least half -true. Grandpa Olson's parents were Olaf and Maria (nee Persdotter) Peterson, who were born in Varmland Sweden in 1823 and 1822, respectively, and they emigrated to America in 1881. Much more about the Olson family is revealed in the chapters that follow.

The Norwegian side of my family is revealed in excellent records kept by Ann Pederson of Willmar. My maternal grandfather's name was Julius Pederson (son of Peder Olson—note the Olson!—Petterud and Maren Brededotter.) Julius was born in Brandvall, Solor, Hedmark, Norway in 1859 and came to America in 1889. My maternal grandmother was Maren Martinsdotter Mengland of Solor, Norway (daughter of Martin Jonson Mengeland and Karen Kristiansdotter). She was born in 1865. He was 31, and she, 24, when they immigrated.

They settled on a farm near Spicer, Minnesota, and had 10 children: Martin(1890-1974), Clara (1891-1977), Oscar (1893-1961), Agnes(1894-1960), Arnold,(1897-1918, Albin (1900-1978), Mabel (1903-?), Rueben(1905-1980) Esther (1907-1999), and Joseph, who was stillborn, is believed to have been the sixth child. Arnold died in the flu pandemic. Julius and Maren were married for over fifty years. He was 81 when he died and Grandma Pederson was 75.

Future generations will continue to contribute to the human gene pool, as did generations before us. We are human and we are Americans, sharing our ancestry, our history, backgrounds, and our culture. We know there is scientific data that traces all known life forms to a single ancestor that lived more than 3 billion years ago. And the fact is, DNA is renewable and can survive unchanged from hundreds of millions of years ago. With this knowledge, we descendents of Carl and Carrie Olson can be proud to have contributed our good genes from our Swedish ancestry to successive generations of living bodies.

The Carl and Carrie Olson home. Standing in front are the two sets of twins, Cecil and Stanley, center, born in 1902, and Parnell and Parker, born in 1912.

Prologue

From Sweden to America

With good land like this, he'd never have to suffer the way he had in his godforsaken homeland. They were really "dirt poor" back in Sweden, Carl Olson told his sons, quickly reminding them that it wasn't because he and his family didn't work hard. It was all those years of poor harvests—everybody was starving. There just wasn't enough tillable land for the growing population.

Fortunately, Minnesota was hungry for people. The state had been urging Scandinavians and Germans to consider America. The Minnesota Territory offered rich and affordable farmland, made available for settlement through America's Homestead Act of 1862. And there were employment opportunities in the timber and mining industries, and the railroad. Thousands of Scandinavians had already emigrated, some leaving as early as 1840.

The Swedish people thought there should be only one kingdom on the Scandinavian peninsula. At the time Carl Olson came to America, Oscar II was the king of the two countries. Conflicts had persisted between Norway and Sweden for more than 90 years with all attempts to forming one nation failing. King Oscar II allowed each country to have a parliament of its own and no Swede held office in Norway, and no Norseman had any in Sweden. The only offices open to citizens of both countries were the diplomatic and consular services. The Swedes looked down on the Norwegians, and in 1905 King Oscar II repealed the Act of Union and also abdicated his throne in Norway.

Farming and fishing were the main occupations in Sweden and Norway. As the population grew the number of small farms increased with the amount of tillable land averaging less than ten acres. Farmers found it difficult to make a livable income. There was religious discontent. Many Swedes were objecting to the practices of the state's church, which were based on Martin Luther's teachings.

Carl recalled that pamphlet he had picked up in Sweden many years ago. *Everything in it was true.* Minnesota farmland was flat and fertile and plentiful. There were rivers and many lakes, even a natural spring on his land. It *was* a land of endless opportunities.

He paused, and looked at the shocks of golden grain surrounding him. Then his thoughts went back to that small piece of land in Applebo Forsamling, Dalerna where his family had tried to eke out a living. He smiled, proudly and smugly. It couldn't compare to what he now owned! *It was an amazing country.* It gave him 160 acres for nothing. All he had to do was be willing to settle there and cultivate it for a few years.

Carl spent his boyhood in Sweden. In 1879 when he was 25 he decided to leave his homeland and immigrate to the United States. He spent his entire life in the Arctander township area in south central Minnesota, settling on a farm and homesteading there in 1883. He missed his sweetheart in Sweden and needed her help. Confident, and lonely, he knew it was time to send for Carrie Lofven. Carrie arrived in the spring of 1886; they were married that fall in Willmar.

He was indeed a lucky man. Carrie had given him ten healthy sons; four were in the field with him now. The crop was ready for harvesting. Horses had already pulled the binding machine across the field and cut and tied the grain into bundles that now were scattered across the parcel of land. He and his sons were "shocking," putting the bundles together with the heads of grain toward the sun so they could dry. In a few days they'd pitch the bundles into wagons and haul them to the threshing machine.

There were no easy jobs during the threshing season. Each man had a special task. Some drove wagons, pulled by a team of horses, which hauled the bundles to the thresher. A couple of men had to bag the grain as it came out of the spout. Someone drove the tractor, another tended its boiler, and others hauled grain from the separator to the barn.

The farmers shared their equipment. As soon as they finished the Olson fields, Carl would take his threshing machine, his horses and hay racks down the road to the next farm.

Hot and sweaty, and hungry, Carl leaned on his pitchfork and looked up at the sun directly above him. *Ya, it vas time for dinner, time to take a break.* He called out to his sons. As they headed toward the house, he reminded them that they had to get back out in the field and finish the shocking today. If it didn't rain the neighbors would be there on Monday to start threshing

Most of the Scandinavian immigrants in Minnesota became farmers, settling on undeveloped land. Those who were skilled in trades settled in the larger cities on the east and west coasts. When iron ore was discovered in the northeast part of the state in the 1880s, it attracted immigrants from eastern and southern Europe. By 1900 Duluth had become a major lake port and Minnesota was known, not only for its farming, but it now also became a national iron mining center.

The stern nature of the Old Country gave Carl the characteristics required to meet the hardships he would face in his new homeland. Like most Scandinavians, he had patience and endurance. His hard work and a frugal nature paid off. He was able to buy more acreage. In less than a decade, he became the owner of 320 acres of rich farmland. His farm was probably the largest in the county.

Carl's parents, Olaf and Maria Peterson, followed their son Carl and his three brothers and a sister to America in 1881. They lived with their children most of the time, both dying at 91 years of age.

Carrie had four boys in rapid succession, in 1888,'89,'90 and '91: William, Algot, Hjalmer and Milton, respectively, and then a daughter, Ethel, born in 1892. A fifth son, Elmer, was born in 1894. The very next year, 1895, another son, Walter, was born, and another daughter, Esther, was born in 1900. Families expected their children to help, and Carl was no exception. But life on the farm was hard work, harsh and bleak, compared to city life. No wonder so many young people were leaving the farm as soon as they could. However, Carl was lucky to have more sons to help him run his farm: In 1902 when Carrie was 38 she gave birth to twins Stanley and Cecil, and ten years later when she was 48, she delivered another set of twins, healthy boys, Parker and Parnell.

There was a lot of work to be done on this large farm. The fields had to be planted and harvested. Corn, wheat, oats, rye and flax all grew well in this land. The chickens, geese, pigs, cattle and horses had to be fed. Carl needed to fill the barn with hay for the long winters when snow covered the pastures. The cows had to be milked. The barn and chicken coop had to be cleaned. When a piece of farm machinery broke down, it had to be fixed.

Too much rain or too little rain determined the farmer's success and the livelihood of his family.

Wheat was Carl's primary cash crop. Somehow, he survived the terrible drought in 1888, but faced a season that was far worse in 1930. Besides the problems of drought, Carl and his neighbors saw the railroad rates increasing. They depended on the railroad to take their grain to St. Anthony Falls in Minneapolis, the major U.S. four milling center at that time. Minnesota was considered "the breadbasket of the world." The Midwest had enjoyed bumper crops of grain for years, sending massive quantities of wheat to Europe when their crops failed.

William and Algot were the first to leave the Olson farm and move to Pollockville, Alberta, Canada. When Walter was 14 he joined his older brothers and made his home in Calgary. Hjalmer also moved there and helped his brothers on the ranch for 11 years. Ethel and her husband, William Woldman, moved to Wetaskiwin, Canada in 1932. She died there seven years later at the age of 47. They had no children.

William was called one of "Alberta's plains pioneers." He was a resident there for sixty years, retiring from farming in 1951. William died when he was 81.

Some third generation cousins speculated that William and Algot moved to Canada to escape the World War I draft. However, according to William's obituary, he moved there in 1909, seven years before America's Conscription Act was enacted. During WW I, Algot served in the Canadian Army (or Navy) in Vladivostok, Russia.

All men in the United States between the ages of 21 and 31 had to register for the draft in 1917 and later, in 1918, registration was mandatory for all men between 18 and 45. All had to register, even the blind. Hjalmer and Walter would have been the right age to have gone to Canada to escape the draft, but there is no proof that this is what they did.

Exemptions were granted, but registration was required. Pacifists and Abolitionists were required to report for non-combative service, usually in camps where the conditions were harsh and they were treated poorly. Canada was a popular destination for young men during the Civil War. During WWI Canadians avoided conscription by fleeing to the United States and Americans again fled to Canada.

The Olson brothers' decision to move to Canada may have been have been triggered by their father's demands. Grandpa was a tough boss and farming was hard work with few personal rewards. He would go to bed at 8 o'clock and get up at 5a.m. He called the Knutson farm down the road "Sleepy Hollow" because no one there got up early enough as far as he was concerned.

While freedom and wealth were there for the taking in central Minnesota, it took an oppressive and domineering hand to manage Carl's kingdom of bright and scrappy young men. There was a lot of acreage to care for. Although the house was big enough for the family, there was no electricity or running water. Like their father, it would make sense for the young men to use the skills they had learned on the farm to carve out a future of their own. And they did just that, leaving the farm when they could.

For a farmer's son school was not an option; when it was planting time the boys had to stay home and work. When I was in first grade there were a couple tall, muscular boys who looked too old to be in grade school. They were 15 or 16, in the eighth grade; they hadn't been able to keep up with their schooling because farm chores came first.

Chapter 1

My New Home

We walked up the grassy hill toward this big white house, took a few steps up and through a porch that was cluttered with dirty men's shoes and a box filled with wood. A man that looked like my father opened the door and greeted us. That's Grandma at the kitchen table, my mother said. *This is your new home.*

This house was so big, so different from the home I left. I probably clutched my mother's hand and wondered why we were here. *How could I fly through the air and have Daddy catch me now?* There were only *two steps* into this house, not a steep outdoor stairway to the second floor. I loved sitting on the landing, waiting for him to come home from work. "Catch me Daddy," and then I'd fly when he held out his arms.

It was during the Great Depression, and my father had lost his job with the transit company in Minneapolis and had to return to the farm where Grandpa always needed more help. We would be living with Grandma, Grandpa, Aunt Esther, four of Dad's brothers—including the one who looked like my dad: his twin brother. I didn't know it, but I would soon have a baby brother.

When the first home by the side of the road became too small for the family, Grandpa built the house we now were living in: a two-story, ten-room house on a hill, overlooking green pastureland and surrounded by woods. Grandpa Olson often was referred to as "the richest farmer in Arctander County." He must have been. He drove a big Packard, had a

1

house that looked like a Southern mansion, and Grandma even had a gas-powered washing machine.

One morning I walked into the kitchen and the air was dense, warm and foggy, and then I saw what was happening: Steam from the large copper tubs on the kitchen stove was drenching the air. It was Monday, wash day, and Aunt Esther was filling that big machine that washed clothes with hot water. I watched her. The noisy, rhythmic agitator blades would swish back and forth and wash the clothes automatically and then she'd pick up the dripping item and run it through a wringer. I liked to watch her and wanted to help, but she wouldn't let me put the clothes between the rollers. She said she was afraid I might get my hand caught, but she did let me use the scrub-board. I knew how to do that. That was how my mother washed clothes in the apartment.

A long table dominated the kitchen. The pantry that held all the dishes and food was large enough for my mother and Aunt Esther to work in at the same time. When the wonderful aroma of fresh baked bread filled the air, I could hardly wait for the best treat in the world, even better than ice cream: a slice from the crusty end of a loaf, spread with lots of soft butter and homemade jam. Sometimes I had to wait until it was cool enough to slice, but I knew the rewards of patience. (I still prefer the crust, often tearing away the soft portion from a roll and leaving it on my plate.)

A telephone—too high for me to reach—hung on the wall, next to a big calendar. Whenever it rang, someone in the kitchen would announce *it's not for us* or answer it when it was Grandpa Olson's particular short and long bell tones. I was amazed that all the grownups could tell the difference. Although one could listen in on someone's conversation, I never saw anyone do it.

A dipper that everyone used for drinking hung from the pail of water next to the kitchen sink. Everyone in the family brushed his teeth and washed his hair at that small sink in the corner. One usually had to prime the pump (add some water to expel the air) to activate the flow from the cistern.

I would watch Aunt Esther unwind her tightly-wound golden braids from her head and was surprised how long it was when she washed it. And her mouth foamed when she brushed her teeth. She used tooth paste; my family used soda and sometimes Dr. Lyon's, which never produced a frothy mouth.

My aunt often walked around talking to herself. She seemed angry about something. "Poor Esther," my mother would say. She had "that big house to take care of and all the boys to cook for." Mother said she was going to be "an old maid if she stuck around that house." Esther spent half her life taking care of the large Olson family and the big house— fixing three meals a day, doing the laundry, cleaning the house, gathering eggs, planting gardens, and caring for her sick mother. And all that was before electricity or running water! Her sister Ethel, who was eight years older, wasn't that much help. Her siblings said she had never been strong or healthy. Ethel was only 20 when she got married and left the farm.

Aunt Esther showed me how to gather eggs from the hen house. She'd reach into the nests and gently place the fresh eggs in a basket so they wouldn't break. When the basket was full, but with more nests to search, she would scoop up the corners of her apron to create a large well for more eggs. It was fun gathering eggs from the rows of nests in the chicken coop but there were always a few hens that seemed to prefer to lay their eggs in the barn. Whenever I had to check out the barn for eggs I would cautiously reach down into the dark nest in the hay because I never knew what I'd find – maybe a mouse would skitter away, or a spider. I shuddered and pulled my hand back quickly the time I reached down and touched something soft and smooth: an egg without a shell, only a soft membrane surrounding it.

The house was surrounded by oak trees, elms, cottonwoods, sumac and evergreens, a large apple orchard, fields of grain and corn, and several outbuildings, including a barn, chicken coop, granary, a smoke house, and a "machine shop," which had been the original home by the side of the road. Down the hill and through the pasture, small emerald green islands of grass were surrounded by bubbling and flowing water from a natural spring that provided refrigeration for the family, as well as water for the livestock. Much of the land had been cleared for grazing and was now dotted with stumps.

An oval tank with constantly flowing ice cold spring water sat in the pasture, a good distance from the house. It served as the ice box in the summer. The cold water was numbing. If I couldn't immediately find the milk, cream or butter that Grandma or Aunt Esther had asked for, I'd have to withdraw my arm and rub it briskly before reaching down into the water again. When the cattle and the big bull were grazing near the spring Grandma or Aunt Esther would send one of the boys to get what was needed.

There were five bedrooms upstairs and a bathroom with a tub, a toilet and a sink, towels on the rack, and all the fixtures were in place, but nothing worked. I never did see water flowing from the tap. Besides the large kitchen and walk-in pantry, there was a library with a brown leather couch, a large table, and a few books and magazines, mostly Westerns. I'd inhale deeply to take in the scent of leather whenever I walked into the library. Years later when I decided to read the stories my uncles enjoyed I found they depicted cowboys as drifters, but quite likeable, and they typically slept with squaws and whores, but nevertheless, were respectful of women.

The dining room was rarely used and was no more pretentious than a school room. A large oak table surrounded by solid wood chairs sat in the middle of the room. Leaves could be inserted for special occasions. A buffet held the "good dishes," china decorated with roses on the rims, and lids that covered some of the big bowls. Ferns, coleus and other plants lined the wall of windows. Two oval-framed, sepia portraits of two old people, who looked very stern and serious, hung on a wall.

The formal parlor had a burgundy patterned wool rug instead of the linoleum that covered most of the wooden floor in the dining room. The only time someone went into the parlor was when we went in to hear Aunt Esther or my mother play the piano. The room was uncluttered. I didn't like to sit on the sofa with its curved arms and legs and fancy lace antimacassar because the soft-looking horsehair fabric was scratchy on my bare legs. In front of the windows that looked out across the lawn and pasture below there was a round table with a lace doily and an oil lamp that had a peach-colored porcelain base. Resting next to the lamp was a kaleidoscope, which fascinated me as I rotated the tube and watched the colorful beads of glass form different designs.

My favorite times on the farm were when my cousin Shirley (Lu) and her parents, Elmer and Rena, would visit us from Minneapolis. She and I played with paper dolls, each of us taking a stairway, talking to ourselves, laying the paper clothes on the steps. We'd walk down the hallway where our dolls would visit each other. The dolls talked and visited like grownups. *I can't stay any longer. I have to go home and fix dinner. Good bye. See you soon.* Then we'd return to our own stairway home and quietly amuse ourselves, cutting out dolls and clothes from the big out-of-date pattern books my mother got from grocery/department store in Pennock.

Lu and I liked playing outdoors better than paper dolls. We romped around the barn, jumping through the openings in the floor to the hay below, hanging on the ropes that carried the hay, getting on the backs of the calves and trying to ride them. One of us would stand outside the pen with a pitchfork and prod the calves' hoofs if they wouldn't move.

We asked Uncle Stanley if we could ride in the manure carrier and he cleverly said, "You have to clean the barn first." So we did. We changed our mind when he reminded us that the carrier on the conveyor belt automatically tipped over when it reached the end where there was a big, smelly pile of manure with thousands of flies swarming around it. We contemplated jumping out before the end, but it was way too high above the ground.

The big toilet in the woods with its four holes, varying in size to safely seat little children and adults, was a quiet place where my cousin and I could sit and talk while doing our business. Before using the Sears catalogue we'd close our eyes, tear out a page and giggle if one of us had to use a page that advertised a stove or tool. *Ha,ha, I got nice soft towels!* Sometimes we'd go through the dress section and take turns playing "I get, you get this one." Two little girls who had only paper dolls for toys found many silly ways to amuse themselves.

Although a year younger than I, Lu was the one who decided what we should do. She had such good ideas, I thought. We had been bothered by Benny, one of the boys from another farm. If we were eating Crackerjack or candy he'd grab it out of our hands and run away. One day we were sitting on the edge of the well eating candy and looking at the pale green chicken poop that had hardened from the summer sun. It was quite pretty. It didn't look like what it was. We saw Benny coming. "Here, put the candy in your pocket," Lu said. I did. Then we quickly scooped up some lumps of poop and put them in the empty candy bag and pretended to be eating something sweet and delicious. Sure enough, he came over, grabbed he bag, and ran away. We took off in the other direction, right into the house where our mothers were working in the kitchen. Safe and protected. We heard him complaining to Stanley, but Stanley just told him to leave the girls alone.

The" back stairway" that led to the second floor of the farmhouse was entered through a side door off the kitchen. The other stairway was toward the front entrance of the house, next to the parlor. A black and white china cat rested on the floor near the newel post that supported the varnished oak handrail. One day I was sliding down the smooth and slippery banister and landed on it; it did not survive my landing. I looked at the broken pieces and thought only of running away. I went into the woods and hid. I was scared. But no one was calling my name, nor even looking for me. After what seemed like a very long time, I headed back to the house, apprehensive, unsure of what would happen. I had never been punished or even scolded. I knew I had done something wrong, but I didn't know how to react. It was my favorite uncle, Parnell, who was the first person to say something about the broken cat. "Come here, do you want a spanking?" he asked. But he was smiling, so I obediently walked toward him. He picked me up, put me over his knee, and lay his hand, palm–side up on my rear end, then slapped one hand with other. Clap, clap, clap. He and everyone else in the kitchen laughed. That was it. Nothing else was said. I was only five, but I told him I wanted to marry him when I grew up.

I remember when the uncles would gather around the kitchen table on a Sunday morning to enjoy their beer. The uncles talked and laughed a lot more then. The talk was about crops and politics, which I didn't pay much attention to, but when they told a story and everyone laughed, I tried to remember it so I could re-tell it and have someone laugh at my joke. I guess I found it hard to get attention with so many people in the house. After hearing one of the jokes, I asked my mother, "Do you know what one deer said to the other one?" and she said no and I gave her the answer, "I'll never do that again for a buck." She didn't laugh. She told me not to tell it any more. "It's not nice," she explained. But I did remember it and kept telling it until someone explained it to me – how many years later I don't recall.

Grandpa spoke very little English, but seemed to understand it. He was lean, often wore a suit and tie, limped, and walked with a cane. He was old, in his seventies, and I was almost five when we moved to the farm. I remember he always seemed to be going someplace in his big Packard, and I always begged to go with him. When we went into town, the little village of Pennock, he always bought me a box of Crackerjack.

There weren't many roads in those days. We were returning from Pennock, I, in the front seat, eating my Crackerjack, when Grandpa suddenly steered the big Packard down into a shallow ditch and up and onto a dry, stubbly field. We humped and bumped across the stumps and stalks. I didn't know where we were going, but it was fun being jiggled around in the front seat. I held onto my Crackerjack as if my life depended on it. We finally approached a barn and slowed down. We were at Clifford Lindgren's farm, where there were a lot of kids to play with, a big kitchen, and beautiful pictures on the living room wall that Anna, their mother, had painted.

Threshing season was more fun than going to a carnival. It was an exciting time—different things to do, more talking and laughing. It was like lighting firecrackers on the Fourth of July or playing singing and dancing games at an ice cream social. My uncles would let me ride in the hay rack when they gathered the shocks of grain from the field or in the grain wagon when they hauled it to the grain elevator in Pennock. If I decided to stay indoors during threshing time I'd get to go with my aunt and mother to the fields to take morning coffee, cold drinks, sandwiches and cookies to the crew. Their work started early in the morning, as they had to feed 15 or more hungry men three times a day—sandwiches in the morning, a big dinner at noon, and cold drinks and cookies in the afternoon. The refreshing summer nectar was usually made from Watkins cherry or orange flavored syrup.

The aroma of fresh baked bread greeted the threshers as they approached the house. Sticky fly paper hung from the porch ceiling, successfully capturing many of the filthy insects before they could enter the kitchen. Plates and silverware covered the colorful floral-patterned oilcloth on the extended kitchen table. The cobwebs had been swept away from the outdoor toilet. The hungry men, all in overalls, smelling of grain and dust, would splash cold water on their faces and wash their hands at a makeshift sink set up by the kitchen door. The stand held a metal basin, a big pitcher of water, soap, and a towel.

The dry grain and hay made the body itch. I noticed the sunburnt and sweaty farmer at the dinner table who picked up his knife, reached around behind his neck and under his shirt and unabashedly scratched his back for several seconds. When done, he took the knife and swiped it across his overalls, then reached across the table for a slab of butter for his bread.

I was shocked to see that. I told my dad what he done. He smiled, didn't react, didn't seem surprised, but turned to mother and Aunt Esther with a slight smile on his face told and them what Tina did when the threshers were having dinner at her farm. He said Tina walked around the table with a loaf of fresh bread under her armpit and asked the men if they wanted any bread and if they said yes she just sliced it off and let it drop onto the plate. They all laughed, so I did too. When he told the story, dragging it out like a dirty joke with a punch line, well became *vell*, and just was *yust*. It was the typical Scandinavian accent.

I knew my mother and my aunt would not approve of either scratching your back with a table knife or serving bread the way Tina did. My mother wouldn't allow my dad to sit at the dinner table in his undershirt. *Cecil, go put on a shirt.* She'd tell my brother and me, "Get your elbows off the table." When she was in her eighties she said she didn't think it was right the way some young boys were allowed to wear their caps at the dinner table.

It was not unusual to see guns propped up in the corners of the kitchen during pheasant season when the city folk would come to the farm to hunt. That would certainly be considered negligent action today if there were young children around.

The women in the house were expected to get up just as early as the men—usually before five—to fix a big breakfast that included fried potatoes and eggs. And they took care of the garden, planting potatoes, beets, beans, tomatoes, rutabaga, radishes, carrots, and then found time to beautify the front yard with flower beds. They churned their own butter and canned hundreds of quarts of fruit and vegetables for the long Minnesota winters. The main meal was at noon—dinner time— and that always consisted of meat and potatoes, homemade bread, and a dessert, either cake or pie. In the spring you could count on a delicious fresh rhubarb pie and in the winter, wonderful custard pies.

My only memories of Grandma Olson are when I would sit beside her and she would brush my hair. She spoke only Swedish, was very hard of hearing and always wore an apron over a soft but ample body. I didn't know that she was quite sick at the time and would soon die.

The Olsons never suffered during the Great Depression the way the people in the towns and cities did because they raised their own food: eggs, chickens, geese, vegetables from their garden and apples from the orchard. They milked the cows, skimmed off the cream and churned their own butter. The barn and the pig pen provided the beef and pork they had become accustomed to eating daily.

Many farmers lost their farms after the stock market crash of 1929. They had products to sell in many cases, but no one could afford to buy anything. Corn was selling for less than ten cents a bushel. And if a farmer owed the bank money and couldn't afford to make the payments he went bankrupt, and lost the farm. It seemed natural to get by on very little and not waste anything. Carl and Carrie were fortunate because they had several sons to help them with all the daily chores: milking cows and feeding livestock twice a day, gathering eggs, hauling water, chopping wood, filling the wood box.

After the birth of twins Parker and Parnell, Carrie's health declined and she became quite sick. The task of raising the young boys often fell to their sister Esther, who was twelve years older. Esther remained in the house, caring for everyone until after her mother's death in 1934. According to her obituary, Carrie died of "numerous complications."

As the family grew and left the farm, so did the energy and enthusiasm that had resonated the homestead for almost forty years. What would happen to the farm when Carl died? At age 76, when he was of sound mind and Carrie was alive he made a will leaving the entire estate to her with the provision that the farm could not be sold, but kept intact and not mortgaged. He made a special provision of $2,000 to his daughter Esther. Upon the death of his wife, he bequeathed equal shares to his eleven surviving children. Milton had died in the 1918 flu pandemic.

* * * * *

Before moving to Pennock we lived in a farm house that had some rundown outbuildings and a barn that had housed animals at one time. It would have been a perfect subject for one of Edward Hopper's paintings. The house needed painting, the yard was overgrown with weeds and tall grass, the only sign of life; a few chickens, and Rex, our golden retriever. The land had either been sold or rented out to someone else so my father was a hired hand at another farm, about a mile away. He got paid $18 a month and each day when he returned to our house he'd say, "Well, another day, another dollar."(No wonder I was never good at math!)

Mom knew how to cut hair so it was not unusual to see one of the farmers sitting in the kitchen with a dish towel around his neck. A simple thank you was all she expected, but they usually gave her a pound of home-churned butter or a dozen eggs. *Oh, you didn't have to do that. Thanks a lot.* Mother would boil flax and water to make wave set, then set her hair in deep waves or comb it through my hair before wrapping it around a thumb-sized stick to form ringlets like Shirley Temple's.

When the soles of my shoes wore out my mother would cut out layers of cardboard and that worked for awhile. We played card games, and when the Old Maid deck wore out, Mother would cut out cards from cardboard and make a new deck. I loved running around barefoot in the summer, but Mother made me wear shoes when I stood in line for unmarked canned goods being handed out by the government. *I don't want people to think we can't afford shoes for our kids.*

I started school while at that farm, walking more than a mile to a one-room schoolhouse. I missed a lot of days in the winter because the weather was too harsh to send a youngster out across the snow-swept fields. There was a farm house between our house and the school so sometimes I'd stop there to get warm before going on, taking the snow out of my black rubber, buckled overshoes, and shaking off the ice crystals that had formed on the wool scarf covering my mouth and nose.

I was the only first grader, the youngest and the smallest child in the school. I didn't seem to belong there. I was frightened, too shy to talk to anyone. I ate my lunch by myself. I was glad when it was recess because then we all would go outside and play games. I finally was part of the group. But I knew if they were choosing up sides for some game I'd be the last one chosen.

Some of the boys in the eighth grade were sixteen, or maybe older, because they attended school only when their families didn't need them on the farm. We played games kids still play: Drop the Handkerchief, Red Light-Green Light, Hide-and-Go-Seek. Once when the teacher was inside we were playing Truth and Consequences behind the school, where there were no windows. I had to "pay the consequence," the eighth grader said, ordering me to lie down face-up on the ground. Then Elroy, a second grader, was asked to get on top of me. We did what we were told and everyone laughed. I didn't know why but I suspected from the reaction that it was something we should not be doing.

We had a lot of chickens and they were my pets; when one of them died I took it into the woods and buried it, placing a stone and flowers on the grave, and saying something about "dust to dust." I had been to a funeral and heard the pastor say that. I danced and ran through the empty barn and I tried to create a garden with rocks and flowering weeds in the shallow water of the big round tank where the farm animals used to drink. One day I fell into the tank, but managed to get out and walk to the house. My mother said I was spitting up green slime from the water in the tank. *You could have drowned. You can't play there.* But there was no one to play with. My brother was too young. There were some old automobiles parked on the land and I polished them, slid down the fenders, pretended they were slides, and when I looked at my distorted image on a car door I pretended I was in a carnival fun house.

We didn't see a lot of people, but I recall visiting a neighboring farm when my brother was barely a toddler, handsomely dressed in a crisp white one-piece sailor suit. The neighbor was showing us the garden when I heard LeRoy scream. My brother had reached down to pet the dog and the small terrier had grabbed a chunk of his cheek. The blood was dripping down his face and onto his white romper. I screamed. I cried. He was rushed to the doctor. I don't know how many stitches had to be taken; the scars were visible for years, only recently blending with the wrinkles of age. I will never trust that breed. I prefer big dogs, the Labrador and golden retrievers Dad used for hunting. Too many small dogs seem to have inherited the Napoleonic complex, defending their size by nipping at heels and yapping loudly to announce their ferocity.

An interesting custom took place during the Christmas season, which, if translated, probably would be "Christmas spooking." It sounded like *yula spuking*, as I remember. We would get dressed up in some costume or drape an old blanket over our jackets, wear a mask or paint our faces, and get in a horse-drawn sleigh. A sleighful of kids and parents would ride through the snow, *very* quietly—until we approached a farmhouse! Then we would ring cowbells and make a lot of noise and sing. We'd be invited in for a brief time and the neighbor would try to guess who we were. Once the guessing game was over, we'd remove our masks and the parents would be offered something to drink—usually Swedish *glogg*, a drink as warm as the hospitality. *Glogg* is hot spiced wine and brandy, just the thing for a cold winter night. The kids got cocoa and cookies.

Chapter 2

Cousins at the Farm

Grandpa suffered a stroke in 1938 and now was living with us in the village of Pennock. The younger twins, Parker and Parnell, had left for Chicago to work. Hjalmer was still on the farm, but his health was failing. No one remembered the discussions that must have transpired after Grandpa's death at age 86 in 1940, but the estate was settled and Stanley gave up his turkey farm and returned to the Olson homestead with his wife Bergliot (Belle) and daughter Evonne in about 1945.

Evonne, who was born in 1939, remembers moving to the Olson farm. The Rural Electrification Administration (REA) had already begun bringing power and light to the farms but it was slow in getting power to rural Minnesota. She was "about eight or nine" when electricity finally came to the farm. "How great!" she said.

The tired farm home got a facelift and life was easier and safer with electricity. "We put cupboards in the kitchen. Mom used the pantry for baking . . . and that's where she made head cheese and potato sausage," she said.

"The all-purpose sink in the corner of the kitchen where you washed your hands, brushed your teeth and shampooed your hair, now had running water. Grandpa must have had a vision of things to come when he built the house and put in the bathroom," Evonne said.

However, in the summer there was only cold water flowing through the pipes and the upstairs bathroom wasn't heated so you wouldn't use it in the winter. (Apparently the water heater was turned off in the summer.) The wood burning stove had been replaced with a coal and gas stove that had a hot water reservoir on the side. When Belle wanted to make *lefse*, she would stoke up the coal side and fry it right on top the stove.

"We always got up at 5 a.m. and in the winter we'd fire up the stove with corn cobs and then do our chores," said Evonne.

Evonne slept upstairs and by morning the furnace would be out and "you could see your breath." She'd grab her clothes and rush downstairs to get dressed by the kitchen stove.

The big house, now occupied by a family of three, changed slightly. The library off the kitchen became a bedroom. Stanley now moved a rocker to the sunny dining room where he would sit and read Western stories. The spittoon that had been a fixture in the kitchen when Grandpa and other sons were home now sat near his chair. With all that space available, Evonne used one bedroom as a playroom for her dolls and another room for playing office or school. The third floor attic was another place to explore and she loved to slide down the banister to the foyer.

"It was a house filled with wonderful memories," Evonne said. She loved it when the Chicago relatives came to visit in the summer. They would spend time in the hay mow and the apple orchard. Winters—as were mine—were spent playing cards around the kitchen table. Everyone knew how to play poker, whist, rummy, euchre, Old Maid, Hearts or Five Hundred and bridge was becoming popular. Whist players found a new challenge and a lifelong activity in bridge.

Luckily Stanley never got hit by a train. Evonne said that when her dad came to the railroad crossing, he never stopped, just honked his horn as if he had the right-of-way.

Just because she was a girl didn't exempt Evonne from farm work. She recalled picking up the bales of hay and helping with the harvest, even after her marriage in 1957. Soon the farm got too much for Stanley and he sold it.

There are many lessons learned from living on the farm. While some city kids thought milk came in bottles, Evonne knew where it really came from. She sewed all her own clothes on Grandma's old Singer treadle machine and even made her own wedding dress. When they moved from the farm Belle took the Singer with her and used it until she died, and now Evonne's son has it prominently displayed in his living room. She has Grandpa's seven-day mantle clock, and it still works, chiming on the hour and half-hour.

Remembering Aunt Esther

Esther, the loyal and long-suffering daughter who had taken care of the entire family for so many years said the "good old days" on the farm were really the "hard old days." The daughter who had given up so much for her family had a new role as a wife and mother of two, Richard and Eunice.

Eunice said her mother told her she was named Esther because "her birth date was close to Easter." She also recalled her mother wishing she had had a cookbook back on the farm because she got so tired of making the same meals over and over. It was a meat and potatoes dinner every noon with a cake or pudding topping off the meal.

Richard has some fond memories of farm life. In the summer when he was in high school in Chicago he'd take the Empire Builder train to Pennock to work on the farm of his father's relatives. "Mother always wanted me to go to the Olson farm, but Stanley and Bergliot were awfully quiet and it just wasn't that much fun." But he loved his summers at the Emil Fransen dairy farm. Emil was married to his father's sister.

Scandinavians are typically pretty laid-back and not excitable, and that characteristic was appreciated on a couple occasions.

Richard was 14 when he accidentally dumped a whole load of hay in St. John's Lake. "I had loaded the rack twice as high as I should and I was driving the tractor and my friend was perched on top the hay. The field was rough. . . I turned and the pin popped out of the hitch and the rack slid down a steep slope, right into the lake . . . and there he was, sitting on top a pile of hay in the lake."

The boys drove back to the farm in total silence. "I was scared to death," Richard said. They went to the barn where Emil was milking a cow and told him what had happened. Emil looked up, listened, and calmly said, "Well, you boys will have to get that rack out tomorrow morning," then turned around and went back to his milking. And the next morning, with a little extra help, they were able to retrieve the rack.

Another time Richard was taking a load of grain to the Pennock elevator and misjudged the location of the grain chute. His uncle had told him not to back up with the rig. However, if he drove around the block he'd end up in back of all the other tractors lined up behind him. All he had to do was inch back a little and he'd be in position to allow the grain to flow down the chute. So he put the tractor in reverse, and instantly heard a defiant crunching sound. The draw bar resisted and bent. Now he was going nowhere. He knew his uncle was having coffee at the café so he ran down the street as fast as he could and told him what had happened. Emil hopped off the stool, hightailed it to the elevator, removed the bar, took it to the blacksmith down the street, and ten minutes later they were in business. "Not a harsh word was said. What a great guy he was," said Richard.

Parnell Remembered

Parnell married Gertrude Bendler, and the couple had two children, Karen and Bob. Bob shared some memories of his father: "One thing that I remember, Dad said that it was a big deal to get an orange at Christmas." He also remembered going to South St. Paul with his dad when they bought livestock. Parnell was the "quiet one," and his twin brother Parker was the "spokesman," according to Aunt Esther. Bob said that when Stanley shipped a big carton of eggs to Parnell in Bellwood, Illinois, Dad sent him a postcard, "How much for the eggs?" Stanley wrote back, "Eggs are 10 cents a dozen." There was the usual bartering during the Depression days, but that was the amount Stanley got.

"Parnell also lived in Canada for awhile with one of his brothers (Walter, maybe, or Hjalmer) but one day the brother went to town and made other living arrangements without mentioning it to anyone, and Dad (Parnell) didn't see him until months later when he ran into him," Bob said. From his father, he heard that "Stanley hadn't been able to swallow for years and that Cecil had cancer." (Cecil, my father, had encephalitis in 1941, and many years later he had a pre-cancerous lesion removed from the side of his nose. And I don't remember a time when the two brothers couldn't enjoy a bottle of beer or two.)

Karen had a few recollections of the Olson farmhouse. "I was so impressed with that big house with two sets of stairs." She recalled a story about Grandpa Olson breaking his leg while cutting wood and never having the bone set. Cousin Richard corroborated the story, adding, "He made his own splint because it would have cost $5.00 to have a doctor do it." Karen, too, had heard that Grandpa was "a tyrant" and that's why the kids left home as soon as they could.

Bob and Karen's father, Parnell, was diagnosed with lymphoma in 1974 but managed to work for Babson Bros. Company, manufacturer of dairy equipment, from 1940 until shortly before his death in 1979. He met Gertrude while she was working at Babson. They bought their first house in Bellwood, Illinois in 1945 and moved to Wauconda in 1952.

In 1970 Stanley and his wife Belle and my mother and dad took the train to Chicago to visit Parnell and his family in Bellwood. Parnell, a staunch Republican, was kidding Stanley, "How could a Republican defeat our cousin, Alec Olson, for Congress?" Stanley replied, "Well, there are a lot of dumb people in Minnesota." (Charles Kuralt, (1934-1997), the award winning journalist, known for his long career with CBS, said, "Minnesotans are just different, that's all.")

Alec was a member of Minnesota's popular Democratic Farmer Labor Party. He served in the U.S. House of Representatives and the Minnesota Senate and was the Lieutenant Governor of the State under Gov. Rudy Perpich. Alec's grandfather was Andrew Olson, Carl's brother; their wives, Anna and Carrie Lofven (or Loven), were sisters.

Parnell's twin brother, Parker, was in the army during World War II, serving in Germany and France. He was wounded and received the Purple Heart. After he was discharged in 1946 he went to work at International Harvester in Chicago. He married, never had any children; his wife Anna preceded him in death. An alcoholic, he was living in a transient hotel in Chicago at the time of his death.

Elmer, the "Millionaire"

Elmer probably was the only son before the twins were born who attended school after he was 16 years old. He went to a business school and served in the Army during World War I, and then spent his life working for the post office. He retired to Hawaii and "was a millionaire," according to rest of the family.

"A penny saved is a penny earned" and "Waste not, want not" were adages to live by for Elmer and his wife Rena. Shirley, their daughter, said, "They saved everything, every tiny bit of leftover food." And Rena always found ways to use it, whether an addition to a salad or hot dish. The garbage she wrapped carefully in newspaper, then tied it together with string as neatly as a birthday gift.

"Dad paid cash for everything—cars, house, you name it," she added. "They kept receipts on all their purchases, including groceries." When I was staying with them one summer, I remember borrowing 50 cents from Aunt Rena and she went to a sugar bowl in the kitchen cupboard –her own little bank—gave me the money and put in an IOU. No one in the family called them stingy, just frugal. And they would add, "No wonder he's a millionaire." They were, in fact, quite generous, always bringing gifts when they came to visit, and giving me my first bike when Lu got a new one.

Lu remembers setting up a checking account for her mother after she moved in with Lu and her husband Harvey. "Mother was so pleased with herself when she wrote her first check—one to her sister for her birthday."

Elmer loved gardening, and had a beautiful yard in Minneapolis with a variety of flowers; huge dahlias lined the garage wall and the lawn never saw a dandelion – for long. When we threw a blanket on the lawn for tanning he'd suggest after awhile that we move it so we wouldn't "crush the grass." When they lived by Eagle Lake in Minnesota they had a huge strawberry patch, and visitors always went home with a basket of fresh strawberries when they were in season. When they retired to Hawaii to be near their daughter Elmer added a hot house to his daughter's home and specialized in raising orchids.

Elmer was quiet and gentle, refined, and often had a teasing smile on his face. He would let my cousin and me know it was time to get up by coming into our bedroom and tickling our feet. He had a firm rule: No one could talk when the Lone Ranger came on the radio. I never heard him scold, reprimand, complain or swear. He was much more genteel than my dad and his twin brother, who could laugh at a good story, and enjoy their beer. Elmer would make his own wine and offer it to us when we visited. It was terribly sweet, like Mogen David. Elmer was 87 when he died in 1983 and Rena, who died in 1992, was 99.

Cecil, I Knew Him Well

My father married Esther Pederson of Spicer in 1926. I was born six months later. *You were premature, weighed only five pounds.*

He was a farmer most of his life—working his own farm, someone else's, or managing a turkey farm near Pennock. For awhile he was a rural mail carrier and he kept his .12 gauge shotgun on the front seat so that he could shoot a pheasant if he happened to see one. It didn't matter if it was pheasant season or not; we needed to eat. I also remember seeing him ride one of those little cars on the railroad when he was a gandy dancer, someone who maintains the railroad. He could lay bricks, pour concrete, paint—fix anything!

Dad was a man of few words. Years later when I was married and living in another state I'd call my folks on Sunday when the rates were lower. If Dad answered the phone he'd say, "Yust a minute, I'll get your mother," and put down the receiver immediately. He never lost his Swedish accent—called my first husband Jack, Yak. There also was no letter Z in our house. A button would come loose or one could lose something; both were pronounced like loose. We had haircutting, kitchen and sewing scissors—all pronounced with a hissing sound. That was the way most of the people in this Scandinavian community spoke. I didn't learn "Z" until I took speech in high school. I remember the teacher having me practice the sound: "Buzz like a bee, don't hiss like a snake."

My brother LeRoy was born on the farm in 1931. He served in the U.S. Army during the Korean War. He contracted pneumonia and ended up being sent to Germany from 1952 to 1954, rather than Korea. He married Lolly Peterson when he got out of the service and worked in Minneapolis for six years before taking a civil service test and returning to Willmar to work for the postal department for over 30 years. He and his wife Lolly have two daughters. He is an avid fisherman and hunter, just like our father was.

Lee and I are five years apart, and our personalities and politics are very different. He seemed to get into trouble as a kid, and I admit I knew how to deflect his teasing by yelling, "Mother, he's going to hit me," long before he had a chance to do anything. He was scrappy, ready to take punch at someone when he felt threatened. "When you're small you have to be ready to fight," he said.

Dad was really unhappy with him the time he was throwing a ball and accidentally broke the big window of the butcher shop. Dad was returning from the hardware store where he had paid for a new window when he ran into LeRoy on the street. He reminded him how costly the replacement was and scolded him again for being so careless. Talk about bad timing! Lee was on his way to tell him that he had just tossed a ball to his dog and *it went through the post office window*! Although we were poor, Dad somehow found a way to pay for the windows. Lee may have set some record for breaking windows in his youth. "Another time I was bragging that I was 'King of the Hill' and the kid punched me and knocked me through the plate glass window of the restaurant."

Chapter 3

Growing up in Pennock

Grandpa was pretty much confined to his bed in my upstairs bedroom in Pennock about a year before he died in December, 1940, but he was feisty enough to knock out a window and carry on a conversation, he thought, with President Franklin Delano Roosevelt and even Hitler. He usually mumbled in Swedish, or a combination of English and his native tongue.

My brother and I would sit at the foot of the stairs and listen to his ravings, but we were afraid to go upstairs. We recognized his rantings one time when he screamed, "Adolph, you're going to loose de vor!" When we did see him he was a ghostly, skinny man in long, grayish white underwear and gray hair, bent over with a cane to support him, and to pound the floor when he wanted my mother to bring him something. Dad replaced the window, and covered the bottom panes with boards, and mother covered the upper pane with BonAmi, a pink liquid cleaner that was opaque until removed. I suppose they thought that if he couldn't see outside, he was less apt to try to escape.

My brother and I said he was "crazy." No one talked about dementia or explained what can happen to the mind as it ages. That lesson came more than 65 years later when my own husband suffered from Alzheimers, a disease slowly altering and destroying the mind of a brilliant man.

During the times my Swedish grandfather and my Norwegian grandmother lived with us I picked up a lot of the two languages. I was able to understand and speak them a little, always mixing the two languages in my sentences. There is a unique sing-songy rhythm to both of them, with a recognizable inflection and emphasis that the Coen brothers captured well in their movie, "Fargo." But there are a lot of Scandinavians who deny this. "We don't talk that way" they say.

Ya, maybe not. But, you bettcha, you can still pick up the dialect and readily identify it as 'talking Minnesotan.' You could be wrong though. The North Dakota Scandinavians sound the same way.

My father didn't talk a lot, but he was quick to interject a witty comment into a conversation and usually commented on the news of the day while reading the paper. The commentary wasn't directed toward anyone; the room could have been empty. Bald and a typically fair-skinned Swede, there was a serene gentleness and confidence about him. A wry grin often seemed ready to reach a full smile, but it rarely did.

When he heard me constantly telling my tall and skinny nine-year-old daughter to 'put your shoulders back' his farm-spun wit came through: "Yust let her be, she can crawl under da fences eaSier (pronounced with a hissing 'S') that way."

Mother, on the other hand, was lively, fun, creative and sang a lot as she worked around the house. On Saturday afternoon she'd have the radio blaring with the program that had the opera, often singing along, reaching the crescendo of Lily Pons, or whoever was the diva of the day. She was trim, attractive, had dark brown hair and was always busy doing something with her hands: sewing, tatting, crocheting or knitting. Or she was in the kitchen, fixing a meal, baking a pie, and before Christmas she made *fatigmand*, *pepparkakor* and many other ethnic treats. *Lutefisk*, which was considered a Scandinavian delicacy, was made of dried cod fish pickled in lye, and it was the traditional Christmas Eve dinner. The story was that the cod would sit in barrels of lye outside the butcher shop and men would pee in it. I don't know about that but the mention of *lutefisk* usually draws a look of disgust and some exclamations of "yuck!" My mother's word for something she didn't like was *ishda*. But she would not have *ishda'd* the *lutefisk* dinner; it was a treat, always served with a creamy sauce and other special foods—all heralding Christmas Day, *when Jesus was born in a manger in Bethlehem*. It was a night we thanked God for our food. A night when Santa would fill our stockings. The air was heavy with the scent of pine. We had decorated the tree earlier and tonight we would be able to light the candles. We all sat and looked at the beautiful tree, never taking our eyes off the burning candles. It was tense. We were told the tree could burst into flames if a candle toppled.

When the wood-burning stove was replaced with a gas model Mother complained that she just couldn't make *lefse* any more. The Scandinavian flat bread, which resembles a large tortilla, was made from cold mashed potatoes, eggs and flour, then flattened with a rolling pin and browned on the lids of the stove. You can still buy it at some grocery stores. We ate it with butter and sugar or jam, but it could be used they way pita bread is used in today's popular Mediterranean roll-up sandwiches.

Now that we were living in Pennock Dad didn't have to get up at dawn to milk the cows any more, but old habits die slowly so he was usually the first one up in the morning. He'd make the coffee and take a cup to my mother in the bedroom. If she didn't get up to fix his breakfast, he'd go into the kitchen and have a piece of cake or pie that mother had fixed the day before. He expected mother to fix dinner and supper. He'd be poised at the kitchen table, a knife in one hand and a fork in the other, ready to dig in as soon as she put the meal in front of him. When he was done he pushed the plate toward the middle of the table, making room for the pie, cake or pudding that was dessert.

When I asked my dad about his education, he said, "I tink I finish eight grade." But I also remember one night when I was struggling with homework and Dad came into the room and asked why I was up so late. I told him I couldn't figure out an algebra problem. "Vat is it?" he asked. I gave him the problem. He smiled, and with a slight chuckle, and a dismissive hand, he immediately gave me the answer. I don't remember the problem, but I remember putting down the answer and going to bed. The next day when the teacher asked who had the answer I raised my hand. It was right. But now I was I was terrified that she would ask me to go to the blackboard and show the class how I arrived at the answer. Fortunately, she called on someone else.

Mother and Dad danced well together, sometimes taking my brother and me with them when they went to the dance pavilion in Spicer, a nearby town. There were other kids sitting around watching their parents do the polka, fox trot, schottische and waltz; sometimes one of the kids would get up and dance and act silly, but most of time we just sat there, clapping our hands and bobbing our heads, waiting for mom or dad to swing by. I'm sure we must have complained at times and said, "I wanna go home," but my memories of those times are only pleasant ones.

I was married and had four children when mom and dad flew for the first time to visit me at my new house in South Bend, Indiana. They knocked at the door and I was so excited to see them. Dad gave me a quick hug and hello and without hesitating he asked, "Do you have an oil can? This door squeaks." If something needed fixing, he knew how to fix it, and did it. He rarely got excited and if he did, it was punctuated with a "Yesus Christ!"

I was never punished – probably because I didn't need it! The cloud of threats was sufficient. Before Christmas it was *Santa* who knew if I had been good or bad, according to my mother, and I knew how Santa could punish me. I didn't want a stocking full of coal. My folks never used the "God can see you" threat but my aunts, my friends and, of course, the Sunday school teacher and the minister, told us that, so I thought it was true.

My aunt Agnes told me that if I did something bad I would go to hell, and I asked her what heaven and hell were like. I apparently could be quite irreverent at an early age because when she got through telling me how heaven was beautiful with all kinds of flowers everywhere and hell was a fire, I said I thought hell sounded more exciting. I usually obeyed my parents; I don't remember many *don't* and *you can't*.

They gave me a lot of latitude when it came to making decisions and they trusted me and I never wanted to betray that trust. One night when I was about 10 or 12, I was out riding my bicycle and didn't show up until way after dark. My mother was upset and said, "I'm going to tell your father when he gets home." If she couldn't handle this herself it had to be serious. I heard her tell him the story when he got home and he headed upstairs toward my room. However, being forewarned, I had already found a good hiding place: a big box in the closet that held winter blankets. He looked and looked for me, called my name. I held my breath and didn't move as he ducked to get into the closet under the slanted roof. I heard him leave and head downstairs. He couldn't find me! (Yeah, right! He was probably relieved that he didn't have to administer some punishment. He just wasn't the punishing, scolding type.)

The only time my mother really got angry with me was when I was sent to the store to buy kerosene and sugar. She was using the kerosene stove in the summer kitchen (an area before you entered the house) for canning. This helped keep the rest of the house cooler. She had run out of kerosene and sugar and I went to the store, but I carried them home in one hand so the kerosene on the outside of the can seeped into the cloth bag of sugar. It was the first time I had ever seen her angry. She screamed, "You could have just as well thrown money into the toilet."

She did have a slender switch that she threatened to use, but never did. She sometimes brought it out and issued threats when my brother and I got into an argument. He was a terrible tease. And he said I provoked him, that I started it. It could have been the day he threw a fork at my hip like a javelin when she threatened to get the switch. Apparently the switch, a tender growth that shot off a tree, had disappeared from it hiding place. In his typically smart-alecky style, Lee quickly obliged her threat by running outside, cutting a switch from a tree, and handing it to her. She didn't use it.

I remember asking for ice skates for Christmas when I was in fourth grade and Mother told me they couldn't afford them. I didn't expect to get them but that Christmas I was pleasantly surprised when I received a pair of black leather, size six tube skates. I tried using them like figure skates by pushing the sharp pointed blades into the ice but the boys on the rink told me I couldn't do that because I was creating big gouges in the ice. Because they were so big for me, they offered little support. Hard as I tried, I practically skated on my ankles. I even stuffed cotton in the toes. They were the only skates I ever owned. Nearly twenty years later when my own children went skating I decided I'd go with them. Even with a pair of wool socks, my old skates fit me perfectly. But I heard, "Mother! You can't wear *black* skates!" So I took out the white shoe polish and tried to paint them white like theirs. It didn't cover black leather very well; I should have used house paint.

Mother kept the outdoor toilet spotless and decorated it with pictures and sometimes branches of lilacs or other flowers. However, the trek to the outdoor privy was often challenging. The Forsberg boys next door loved to throw rocks or snowballs (in the winter) at me, hoping I'd pee in my pants. It often took their mother or my mother to get them to stop.

In the winter we had what mother called "The Pail" that we could use. It was our indoor toilet, a big white enamel chamber pot with a lid that was hidden in the closet. We never had indoor plumbing when I was growing up. And this was well into the twentieth century! During the week, we took a lot of PTA baths: pussy, tits and ass! Our bathtub was a large aluminum tub, which we could set up anywhere in the house for our Saturday bath. The living room on sunny Saturday afternoon was my favorite spot for my bath.

When Dad started raising turkeys my little brother would go with him to the turkey farm and drive the truck from roost to roost, sitting on Dad's lap at first so he could learn how to handle the vehicle, then sitting on a pillow so Dad could unload the feed more efficiently for eight thousand turkeys. If a turkey happened to get hit by the truck Dad would bring it home and we'd have a turkey dinner. And turkey sandwiches, and turkey hot dishes, and turkey hash, and turkey soup.

The young boys from town loved it when Dad had to vaccinate all the turkeys for coccidiosis, a highly infectious disease that could kill off the entire flock. He'd hire them to catch a turkey and hold it down while he acted as the vet with his syringe.

An early snow storm before Thanksgiving on November 11, 1940, when the turkeys were fat and ready for processing, killed nearly all the turkeys on the numerous ranches in Minnesota. I remember Dad not coming home all night, working to save as many of them that he could. Those who went to buy a turkey for Thanksgiving that year probably found it very expensive.

Chapter 4

Your Mother's Genes

My mother had taken "a few piano lessons," but she could play *anything*. It was the boogie-woogie era and I turned on the radio and asked her if she could play like *that*. She listened, hit a few keys, and before long she was playing and singing, *It's the G.I.jive, da,da,da dada . . .man alive!*

Almost every night after supper my dad, my brother and I would go into the living room and listen to Mother play the piano. When she played "Napoleon's Last Charge" the room shook. She sounded like Kate Smith, I thought, when she sang

> *When the moon comes over the mountain,*
> *every dream brings a sweet dream of you.*

My brother and I often joined my mother on the piano bench and sang along with her.

Mother's family (the Pedersons), was gifted with musical and artistic ability. Her brothers, Martin, Oscar, Albin and Rueben played the violin, piano and accordion for dance bands into their senior citizen years. Rueben was an accomplished wood carver. He made a Stradivarius-copy violin for himself and platform rockers for friends, relatives and family.

In our dining room there was a picture Mother had painted when she was a girl. It was sunset scene by a lake, with an Indian teepee on one side. I thought it was beautiful and when I asked what had happened to it many years later she said she had tossed it out. "It wasn't any good," she said.

Whenever my daughters and I asked Mother what she wanted for Christmas or her birthday she always said, "Nothing." But she always had something for us—an afghan or doily which she had crocheted, or a pillow that she had embroidered .When she was in her late 80s she wrote the following note inside her Christmas card to granddaughter JoAnne:

> *Another year is soon gone by and I must say I have been staying in the house as I have arthritis in my left leg so I have to lean against the walls when I walk. Don't send me any gifts cause you will get nothing in return.*

> *Lots of love, Gram Olson*

Mother had three sisters, Clara, Mabel and Agnes. As a youngster and a teen-ager I got to know Aunt Agnes well. She and her husband, Ansel Hagstrom, lived in a little house in Minneapolis on Minnehaha Boulevard and had no children. When I stayed with them they would take me to parks, the state fair and restaurants, and they bought me things – candy, ice cream, a new dress. Agnes had a Ouija board and she insisted that she never helped push the wooden device to the right answer. Once she took me to a séance and we played what was called "up table" where the table started to move by itself. Someone tried to contact the dead, but I don't recall any responses, just a few spooky-sounding noises, which seemed to come from the phonograph in the corner. I couldn't figure out what was going on and to this day I don't like magic shows. Although she was the one who had told me about heaven and hell, we never went to church on Sunday. I'd write poems when I stayed with Aunt Agnes and she'd have me read them to the neighbors when they came for coffee. I knew she was very proud of me.

It was like a law: You could never wear white shoes or a white hat after Labor Day in Minnesota. So when Aunt Agnes went to the Minnesota State Fair she made a game of getting rid of her white summer hat. I remember being with her when she removed her hat and hung it on a post and invited me to sit on the bench to see who would take it. "Once a man took it; last year a colored woman did," she said. We were talking and when we looked up the hat was gone. Agnes was fun, interesting, loving, and had many stories. She told me about Buffalo Bill; when she was 15 she left home and went to work for Buffalo Bill's wife in Montana. She said she saw Buffalo Bill only once. He was always on the road with his Wild West show.

Mother was an excellent seamstress who could make me a dress without a pattern. I know I frustrated her when I started to sew my own clothes. Anxious to wear the skirt, I would occasionally use tape to hold up the hem. I got an "A" on the dress I made in home economics class because I stuffed it into my notebook and had Mother fit in the sleeves. She painstakingly showed me how it should be done, easing *thousands* of pins into the opening so that it wouldn't pucker and look like a puffed sleeve. It was an ugly red and white striped seersucker dress that I never wore. I had made a bad choice for a pattern. I should have made an apron like most of the girls in the class did, but I didn't spend a lot of time in the kitchen and I wanted a new dress.

My bedroom had a green floral print bedspread and drapes, all of which she made from flour sacks. I had a lot of clothes and they were current styles, the kind of skirts and dresses the smart and popular girls in school were wearing. Aunt Agnes, who worked for a wealthy family in Minneapolis, would send us dresses and coats the family no longer wore and Mother would rip them apart at the seams and make something new. She even made suits for my brother.

As a youngster I was always writing or drawing. I was about seven when I watched the brilliantly-colored flames lick the sky from a burning barn; I couldn't wait to get home and take out my crayons to capture the colors and the scene on paper. Now I carry my camera with me at all times so I'm always ready for a beautiful sunset or some scene that I can paint. I have painted and studied painting all my life. Painting opens your eyes to the beautiful world around us, makes you aware of reflections, light, and the beauty in a dead tree, or a dark and threatening sky. Look closely at a tree with its rough bark and winding boughs and branches, and its intricate pattern of leaves, and you'll experience the mystery of the universe. Look at a sunset to feel a connection with something that is beyond our comprehension.

Artist Georgia O'Keefe visited northern New Mexico, fell in love with the landscape and never left. Her beautiful striated mountains of various hues—from green to reddish tones, black, purple, rust and brown—look surrealistic, but they are as real as her sensual flowers. I've seen them. I've tried, without success, to paint them as well as the amazing O'Keefe.

My passion for art paid off when I had kids. Carol was about six when we were in a museum and she tugged at my skirt, started jumping up and down, screaming, "Mommy, Mommy, look over there, there's a Modigliani!" She was right. There, across the room, were those Modigliani eyes. She was about two when I gave her a brush to paint with while I was painting and that wasn't such a good idea because she thought the paint tasted good. She has a lot of artistic talent, and expresses it in water color paintings, stained glass, Christmas ornaments, jewelry, and in cooking and baking. Her beautiful fruit tarts look as if they came from a bakery and the pastry-covered whole salmon she fixed for a dinner was a culinary masterpiece, delicious and beautiful with crisp, flakey sculpted fins.

Daughter JoAnne was into cats, drawing cats instead of people— her escape from what would now be called a dysfunctional family. I recognized her cat picture hanging on the wall during the kindergarten open house before Thanksgiving: Several cats, wearing tall pilgrim hats, were seated at a long table. In the center on a large platter was . . . a big, fat, stuffed mouse! With large rolls of paper from the butcher shop she created a symphony orchestra with cats playing the various instruments. She was seven when she filled a notebook with a story about Loretta and Jerry, two cats who behaved a lot like her family. (Not good. The cats argued a lot.)

Nan has taken her interest in art to the classroom, volunteering her time to teach youngsters about photography and painting. She is an interior designer now, a job she loves, and seems to have a natural talent for it. She walked into my house shortly after I had moved into my little condo and took one look at my buffet against the wall and said, "We need to put that at an angle." It was amazing how it much it improved the room.

Typical of my supportive aunts and my mother, they said I was as good an artist as my cousin Lu. I knew better. She could draw and was illustrating for Dayton's catalog when she was in high school. She spent most of her life as a fashion illustrator in Hawaii. She was like a sister when we were growing up. She had class and I was the country bumpkin. She'd visit me and would always bring me something that no one in Pennock would be wearing–like a lace fascinator or a turban to wear on my head. I never did see anyone else in Pennock with one of those, but I knew they were what the girls in cities were wearing and I wanted to be like them. Tall, thin and attractive, Lu could wear pink, orange and purple together and look like a fashion model.

Do you know someone who makes you feel better and makes you want to be a better person after you've spent time with him or her? That's Lu. She never complains, is always upbeat. She has had a double mastectomy, three knee replacements, and been undergoing chemo for cancer year every couple years for more than ten years. (In 1997 she had surgery for ovarian cancer.) She says, "No problem, I just have chronic cancer." I am indeed fortunate to have her living near me.

When we get together we never run out of conversation, laughing at the silly things we used to do. Both of us were flat-chested when we were teens so we'd cut a sanitary pad in two and stuff it into our bras to give us some boobs. Once we stuffed the pads into our bathing suits, and we looked pretty good, we thought, but the pads floated away as we swam. We retrieved them as fast as we could, hopefully before the boys on the beach would see them.

When my folks weren't in the house Lu and I would take my Dad's cigarette papers and can of Red Velvet tobacco and roll our own cigarettes. Then we'd lift the lid from the wood-burning stove, lean down and light our misshapen cigarettes. We coughed, blew smoke, and pretended we were really cool—even though we occasionally singed our hair or eyebrows. (*Cool* wasn't the word then, but we thought we were *something*, sophisticated, like a movie star.) My Big City Cousin was the leader and I, the follower, the imitator, her great admirer. I knew I had a lot to learn.

She took violin lessons and sometimes when she was supposed to practice but wanted to do something else we would go to her room, close the door, and then she would give me a dime to rub the bow across the strings. Her mother never seemed to notice the difference.

Chapter 5

Old Pennock

My grade school, a post office, a grocery/department store, a creamery, an implement shop and a shoe repair shop lined the main street of Pennock. It had a population of less than 500. (Some say I was counting the chickens. The 2008 census was below 500.) It was comfortable and safe and the people were white, Lutheran and predictable.

The women wore cotton dresses and aprons and knew how to bake delicious pies, cakes and cookies. The men worked in the town at the stores, the implement shop, the creamery, the garage or filling station. Everyone ate lots of meat; families rented a frozen food locker in town and every part of the animal that had been butchered would be eaten. The pig's head had already been made into head cheese and the feet had been pickled, and then there was blood sausage, which I never would try. Everyone had peas and carrots for dinner, except in the summer when you could get fresh corn on the cob. You didn't have to buy corn,you just stopped at a farmer's field and helped yourself if you didn't have sweet corn in your own garden.

If you went to church on Sunday it was at the Mamrelund Lutheran church, the only church in town. Blacks were "colored people" or "niggers"— we didn't know any better and I had never seen one. We played games, and determined who was "it" with "eenie, meanie, mini, moe, catch a nigger by the toe, and if he hollers, let him go, O -U -T, spells out goes he/she." We knew there was one Catholic in town and she had to go into Willmar to go to church. Jews? In Sunday School we were told Jesus was a Jew and we didn't know what that was. But from the pictures in our Sunday School books Jesus looked a lot like my uncles, except for the long hair and robe. Although Willmar High School was the biggest high school in the area, I never saw a black there. Someone said Jews ran a little fresh fruit and vegetable store in downtown Willmar. I went into it one day—out of curiosity. They had dark hair, like mine and my mother's, and were pleasant, and the apple I bought was delicious.

You didn't hate anyone because they looked different from you. We all looked pretty much alike--blond, blue-eyed, fair-skinned, a few brunettes. I had one friend who was a redhead.

Most activities took place at the church. The kids went to Sunday School and played games in the basement and there were ice cream socials in the summer that everyone loved. Besides getting ice cream, we'd play games and dance around in circles, holding hands. It was one of the few opportunities to hold the hand of a boy that you thought was cute. Once in awhile we had some *real live entertainment* at the old town hall south of Highway 12. I recall seeing a Charlie Chaplin movie and Our Gang comedies, a hypnotist, and there was always someone selling a wonderful elixir in a bottle that cured everything from the common cold to lumbago.

We could hear the grinding noise and see sparks fly from the blacksmith shop down the street behind our house. The barber shop had a public bath where you could take a bath for 25 cents. There weren't many teens to hang out with but when we did it was to have Coke at the only café in town.

The bank downtown issued driver's licenses. When I was 15, I just walked in and told them I wanted a license and got it. I didn't really know how to drive. I had backed the car out of the garage and driven around town with my cousin a couple times when dad wasn't around. I didn't realize that brakes should be used to *slow you down* and not just *stop suddenly* so we drove slowly, coasting around the corners, slamming on the brakes only when we wanted to stop. Once we swept up and around someone's lawn and hoped no one saw us. When my dad contracted encephalitis and was hospitalized in Willmar, seven miles away, my mother, who didn't drive, wondered how she would get to the hospital to visit him. "Well, no problem, Mother, I know how to drive." She believed me. Let's just say, I got us there and back but she never asked me to drive her there again. Those darn corners kept giving me trouble. I'd take my foot off the gas pedal and try to slow down before spinning around the corner, barely missing the parked cars. I can still hear her shriek, "Dolores! Dolores! You almost hit that car!"

Our house was small with only two bedrooms. Grandma Pederson lived with us before she died, and a few years later, Grandpa Olson spent his last few years with us. When they were with us, I gave up my bedroom to them and slept on a cot in the dining room. Grandma was bedridden, and spoke only Norwegian. When I went upstairs to visit her we just sat and held hands and smiled at each other. We had visited Mother's parents in Spicer many times. As a youngster I remember asking for scissors so I could cut out the paper dolls in the Sunday paper. No, that was a sin, according to Grandma Pederson, but she allowed me to take the paper home so I could cut them out the next day. Grandpa Pederson always said grace before we could eat, and it lasted a long time. It was in Norwegian and I didn't understand any of it but I heard all our names mentioned at one time or another. At the Olson house my father had a short prayer in Swedish that he would recite if asked. I found out some years later that it translated to "In Jesus name, we ate and drank 'til we nearly split."

One reason people left the Scandinavian countries was religious persecution. If that had been Grandpa and Grandma Olson's reason for leaving it would have been because they weren't religious—at least I never knew of them attending church on Sunday or talking about God. My Dad rarely went to church—only to see me perform in a play or sing. Mother went once in awhile and enjoyed the Ladies Aid Society. The church was like the "Y," it was where we went to Sunday School, but it also was a meeting place for all the community. After I was confirmed I taught Sunday School for awhile, but the Bible stories I told the kids just didn't seem plausible to me. The little kids liked them. But they were just that: stories, like fairy stories, I decided.

Chapter 6

High School Days

"Drink this," Mother would say when I was late and racing out the door to catch the bus to high school. It was a beaten egg in a glass of sweetened milk. I'd gulp it down, knowing that it was good for me.

There were usually six or seven of us waiting for the bus in front of the post office and if you weren't on time the bus would leave without you. No parent was going to drive you the seven miles to high school so you'd either stay home and get yelled at for missing the bus or you'd head down to Highway 12 and hitchhike to Willmar. There was no one around to drive you. Even if the men hadn't taken the car to work most of the women were like my mother, they didn't know how to drive.

There were a lot of "snow days." The city kids still had to go to school but we who took the bus got to stay home because the driver couldn't make it through the unplowed country roads. On those days, we'd have long Monopoly games at someone's house or clear off the ice rink for skating.

I had been earning money since I was 10 when I would pick up a small bundle of Minneapolis newspapers at the depot, where the train had dropped them off, and deliver them to a few people in the village. Sometimes there was an extra paper in the bunch and I could take my time to read about interesting things that weren't in the Willmar paper, for example, the sexual exploits of Charlie Chaplin, Errol Flynn and Mae West. On a few occasions when it was really cold Dad drove me around my route and as soon as my brother was old enough to deliver papers, he took over the job.

I was only 13 years old when I began writing a weekly column for the *Willmar Daily Tribune*. It was my job to report all the social activities that happened in the town and the newspaper would print the items in a column titled "Pennock." I loved writing, and I thought I must have been pretty good at it because nothing was changed when I sent the article to the paper. I got paid three cents an inch, and it didn't take me long to realize that I could make more money if my sentences were longer. If I wrote about someone's birthday party, I wouldn't say "She received many gifts." I thought I was pretty clever, saying, "She received many remembrances of the occasion." Hey, those words added up! I couldn't tie up our telephone party line so every Saturday I went from door to door and asked my neighbors if they had had any parties or out-of-town company. They always tried to think of something that would get their name in the paper and always offered me a cookie or donut.

I remember coming home from confirmation class one Saturday and seeing smoke pouring out of our school. I could hardly wait to tell my folks. And even more exciting, I had a real story for the newspaper, not just society stuff. I called the paper and said the school was on fire. But I had no more information. I couldn't answer any other questions. They realized they couldn't count on me for a story and politely said they would handle it. I wasn't aware of the importance of the who, what, where, when and why of reporting. Before the new school was built in 1942, the first four grades met in the old pool hall on the main street while fifth through eighth graders went to an old church several blocks from the old school.

When I took journalism as a sophomore I soon learned that my flowery language was not good journalism. I was the editor of the high school paper in my junior year and I edited the yearbook in my senior year. I loved doing it, although it meant staying after school and taking the train home at midnight. I also was in the junior and senior class plays and those rehearsals were always after school or at night. On some occasions I'd stay with a friend or a relative in Willmar, but studying at the Willmar depot during my junior and senior years was just a normal part of my day. The agent at the Pennock depot was always there when I got off the Great Northern after midnight. I would walk down the dark streets and alleys toward my home, brush my teeth, and quietly slip into bed so that I wouldn't awaken my parents and my brother.

Riding the train was fun. It was during the war and there were always soldiers and sailors on board, going somewhere. The short trip didn't give me much time to meet anyone, but one night I struck up a conversation with a Southern boy on his way to a Reserve Officer's Training Camp in Fargo, North Dakota, and he promised to call and visit me when he could. I could hardly wait to tell my best friend. Alice asked, "What if he calls? "What will you tell your mother?" We walked and walked, trying to think up a good story. We lingered over a Coke at the drug store, pondering what my parents' reaction would be. We finally decided we were probably worrying needlessly. That cute Southern boy named Rusty probably would never call.

But he did call and I tried to sound casual when I said, "Mother, this boy I met wants to come and visit us next weekend. Is that okay?" She said yes, as if I were asking her if my cousin could come for the weekend. There were some questions later, but it just wasn't a big deal. Dad even gave him the use of his car to go to the beach. I liked lying next to him on a blanket near the water and wanted to be closer to him. I had never felt like this before. Hugging him felt good. It was a different feeling, not at all like when my Mother or Dad or aunts and uncles hugged me. But Rusty stopped abruptly in the midst of one of our embraces and raced into the cool, clear water of Green Lake.

I have no idea why I was such a joiner in high school. If there was a club to join, I was in it. I was in radio workshop, where I learned that there was a Z sound in the English language; the Junior Red Cross, where I got sent to a Midwest Junior Red Cross summer camp and missed a lot of activities because I wrote and printed the daily newsletter; choir, where I had to move into the tenor section because so many of the boys were away in the service. I was a constant honor roller, a member of the National Honor Society, class secretary, a member of student council. I was nominated for prom queen and knew that was because I was so active in school. I certainly didn't consider myself pretty or queenly. Neither did the student body. I knew I wasn't friendly and popular like Anna Mae, but I did hope that I would make the queen's court. Of the five candidates, two of us would be losers, and I was one of them.

In those days we didn't think twice about hitchhiking home from school. It made sense because it took an hour to get home via the school bus; we were the last ones dropped off. I never hitchhiked alone. A girlfriend and I would stand on Highway 12 in Willmar and raise our thumbs and usually a local farmer would stop and offer us a ride. He often knew our folks. Once we turned down some guy dressed in a suit and tie because he looked *too slick*.

The three cents an inch I made from writing my column and baby-sitting at 25 cents an hour gave me spending money. Minneapolis was 100 miles away but it was where my cousin lived and life was a lot more exciting in the big city. She'd invite me to join her and her friends for special events; I often bought a ticket on the Greyhound bus and spent the weekend with her. We went to the Prom Ballroom in St. Paul and listened and danced to the big bands, like Cab Calloway, Xaviar Cugat, Jimmy Dorsey and Stan Kenton. I remember seeing Paul Robeson in "Othello" during one of my visits. She introduced me to her friends, and they became my friends. Once we chose to sleep on an old mattress in the attic so we wouldn't have to keep our bedroom neat. We'd slather our bodies with baby oil and spend all day in the sun at Lake Nokomis, trying to see who could get the tannest. She always won.

Lu and I would spend summers together. She loved visiting the farm and the small town of Pennock and I loved spending my summers in Minneapolis with her. The summer after graduation a girlfriend and I packed our suitcases and hitchhiked to a lake cottage in Nisswa, Minnesota, over 100 miles north of the Twin Cities. About eight of us girls, including my cousin Lu, went up there for a week's vacation. We were too young to drink, and I didn't, but I don't recall even being carded—and I have always looked young for my age, something I didn't appreciate at the time. I wanted to look older. I didn't like my round, baby face. We would swim and sit in the sun all day and then get dressed up to hitchhike to the Bar Harbor night club every night to meet boys and dance.

One night a nice looking boy offered me a cigarette, and I said thank you and put it into my mouth, although I didn't smoke. No problem, I thought. I had seen others smoke and even taken a few puffs when I was a kid. He lit my cigarette and I held the smoke in my mouth for a few seconds then slowly let it drift out and wave across our faces as I talked. I didn't think of blowing it out. He looked at me through the cloud of smoke between us and asked, "Have you ever smoked before?" Of course I said yes, but I was so embarrassed. How could he tell? I wondered.

During the summer of 1943 Lu and I took the street car across the bridge to work at the Ford plant in Highland Park, St. Paul, which now was manufacturing defense products. I'm not sure what our contribution to the war effort was, but we sorted parts as they came down an assembly line. The job paid well and we could talk and laugh, within reason, while working. We both were car hops in the evening during the summer of 1944 and Lu also worked full-time as an artist for Dayton's department store. I worked at Sheltering Arms Hospital, a hospital for polio patients. That was a fun summer, especially working as a car hop. A lot of cute guys came to the Richo Root Beer stand and there was a race among us young gals to see who could wait on them. Darn it, I would mutter to myself if I was taking a family's order just when a convertible with some young guys drove in.

We had heard some of our friends talk about French kissing, and wondered what it would be like. So one day Lu and I decided to put our tongues into each other's mouths and were repulsed. Yuck. We just didn't understand what that was all about.

The summer after I graduated (1945), I operated a switchboard for the Air Transport Command at Wold Chamberlain Field. That was the summer I blew some money on flying lessons because I had a crush on a good looking instructor. He paid no attention to me so I took only two lessons. When there was a party at the base I invited Lu to come along. Living in south Minneapolis, it was a short streetcar ride to Wold Chamberlain. For a kid fresh off the farm I was pretty shocked when someone actually threw his glass into the fireplace – just like out of an F. Scott Fitzgerald novel. I learned to drink whiskey sours; they tasted okay, I thought, but before long I felt sick. I realized I had to go to the bathroom and throw up. Vomit breath does not make a good impression, so we got back on the streetcar and headed home and never really had the chance to meet anyone.

The four years of high school went by rapidly and enjoyably. I knew one thing though: I was going to college, no matter what. I knew my parents didn't have the money to send me there but with the summer jobs, baby sitting money and my column I had enough money for my tuition at the University of Minnesota. I could always work and make enough money for living expenses and books, I knew.

Chapter 7

The University of Minnesota

The fall of 1945 I rented a room on campus, paid my tuition, bought my books, and figured I could live on about 30 cents a day for food. White Castle hamburgers were delicious and only a nickel. Once in awhile I'd get a letter from my mother with a five-dollar bill in it. Dad probably didn't know she did that. He wouldn't waste his hard-earned money on a daughter who had these crazy ideas about going to the university. I'd just get married anyway. My parents were always supportive of what I did, but that attitude toward girls was the popular one at that time.

My room overlooked the Mississippi River and two other girls had a room next door. Once I asked them if I could borrow a Kotex pad and they said they only had tampons. I said I couldn't use one because I was still a virgin. They laughed. I couldn't imagine where I would insert it and they assured me that if I tried hard enough I would find the spot.

Later I moved to a house closer to the campus that housed a dozen girls on one floor. We had a kitchen and *one* bathroom, but we seemed to manage nicely most of the time. I didn't do much socializing or partying because I had to work.

I did, however, learn how to smoke correctly that fall. Joyce, a petite brunette with a lively personality and a knack for dressing smartly, gave me the lesson: "Get in bed first because you might get dizzy when you inhale." So I sat in bed and smoked and inhaled, hoping I could become as worldly and sophisticated as my friend Joyce. It was a good thing I was in bed because I *did* get dizzy.

I had a lot of part-time jobs, even folded clothes at a laundry. Chicago author Studs Terkl wrote a book (*Working*) where he interviewed people who held factory jobs and did work that was repetitious and boring. He talked with a woman who folded clothes in a laundry and asked her if they had ever had men working there. She said, "Yeah, we had one once but men just can't seem to fold clothes and talk at the same time."

At the time I was working at the laundry for a few hours in the morning, I also worked at the complaint desk of the Star Tribune after my classes, and on Saturday my cousin and I worked at Bjorkman's, a women's shop in Minneapolis, specializing in expensive designer clothes and furs and frequented by those who had lots of money to spend on clothes. We had to wear black and stand around and wait for customers, who rarely approached us because most of the saleswomen, all older, had their own clientele. We got the curious customers who walked down as far as 10th and Nicollet Avenue occasionally, but they were obviously shocked at the prices and rarely bought anything. Most of the shoppers went to Powers, Donaldsons or Daytons, rarely going beyond 8th Street. When you got to 9th Street you were heading into more expensive shopping territory, like Young Quinlan's, Harold's, and Bjorkman's, way down at the end of Nicollet, not very far from the Basilica.

I remember working behind the purses counter at Bjorkman's one day and a grubby looking guy came in and wanted to look at some bags. I brought out the least expensive ones and he spotted one of the others and asked how much. When I told him it was $300 he said he'd take it and then proceeded to peel off three $100 bills. I remember trying to act nonchalant, as if I wrote up sales like this all the time, but the sale was, I realize, an important lesson in judging people. It's true, you can't judge a book by its cover.

Mr. Bjorkman often used Lu and me for models. I remember when he asked me to put on the chinchilla coat and walk across the street so Mrs. Lampert (of the lumber yard family) could see how "beautiful it is when the sun shines on the fur." The door was in the middle of the street and I started toward the intersection, and he ordered, "No, no, just cross over here." So I jay-walked, something I never would have considered doing on my own.

In l972 when I had my own money and could afford some of the nicer things in life I remember going into a fur store after exercising at the gym. Dressed in a sweat suit and tennis shoes, the saleswoman didn't pay any attention to me when I tried on a $2400 fur jacket. When I took the jacket up to the counter to pay for it the saleswoman asked if I would be putting it on my husband's credit card. No, I said, and took out my own checkbook and wrote a check for the entire amount. She was obviously a little suspicious because she took the check and left the counter to talk to someone in back. The incident made me think of my college days and working at Bjorkman's. It was fun flaunting my independence. My own money.

My cousin was at the University of Minnesota at the same time, and she had a lot of friends. I became part of the group. We would meet every noon at Coffman Memorial Union and listen to petite but curvaceous Dusty with long blond hair tell us about sex. She was the daughter of an Army Colonel and had lived in many places. She was the only one in our group who seemed to know anything about sex. Common words like "come" and "hard on" took on new meanings.

I guess I didn't learn much from Dusty because the first guy who asked me out was Jack, who was in speech class with me, and I didn't handle myself well at all. He was handsome, outgoing, and actually proposed to me in class, which embarrassed me and brought a mild reprimand from the teacher. The subject for discussion was whether college students should marry while in school and he took the affirmative, looking at me all the time.

He would show up at my rooming house almost every night and after a few weeks invited me to have dinner at his house. We had cocktails, I got nauseous and dizzy, and his sister said I should go upstairs and rest. She helped me upstairs and I didn't realize what was happening to me until much later when I woke up and found Jack on top of me. I loved his caresses, but I needed to use the bathroom. The house was quiet. Everyone was in bed. I knew what had happened. I returned to the bedroom and saw the red spot on the sheet. I was no longer a virgin.

It was getting more and more difficult to stay in school. With two jobs, dating, fun with girlfriends and 15 credit hours, something had to go. Once I had lost my virginity, it didn't matter. You couldn't be "almost a virgin" any more than you could be "a little pregnant" and I knew damn well that I didn't want that. First, it would be a disappointment to my family, and secondly, it would destroy my dream of getting a degree in journalism and becoming a foreign correspondent in Russia. It was becoming more and more difficult to resist Jack's passion. He admitted he had "hot pants," and wanted to get married, and I was afraid of getting pregnant, so we decided to get a license and elope. A few nights later, in April of 1948, we drove to Wisconsin and got married by a justice of peace. We weren't going to tell anyone.

But his mother saw the license listed in the paper and now realized she couldn't stop her Catholic son from marrying a Protestant. She wanted me to find a priest, get some instruction, hopefully convert, and then have a wedding. That was a big problem: I was a college sophomore, trying to find the answers to life, and Catholicism was not something I could handle, I knew. *Hey, I don't need an intermediary. I can pray to God directly, and the Vatican telling me what to do? No way.* We went to two priests, including the one at Newman Center at the U, and both of them "flunked" me when I expressed my views about Catholicism. At this rate I would be pregnant before a church wedding! So I said to myself, 'Just say yes to everything, be pleasant, don't argue.' I almost blew it again when we went to Liebeler's church: Father Cogwin politely asked me to sit down and explain my beliefs, and after my explanation he pompously announced, "Well, I've seen other girls come into my office with your ideas but after awhile they have realized that the only way to the Kingdom of God is through the Catholic Church." I stood up, angry, and said, "Father, I will have the decency to respect your ideas if you respect mine." Then I sat down. *Dolores, you can't flunk this priest, just shut up.* I did. I didn't even argue when he said that the two of us would never be together in heaven because there was a higher place for Catholics. *You gotta be kidding. And if we both went to hell, he'd suffer more than I.* These draconian ideas existed in 1948. I had to agree to bring the children up Catholic or he wouldn't marry us. But when it came time to signing the contract I wrote my name in a way that didn't look like my signature at all. It could have been a forgery, I convinced myself.

So, we got married in the rectory, not the church, because I wouldn't convert. No one knew we had eloped three months earlier. We had a small wedding with my cousin and Jack's friend standing up for us and the Liebelers held a lovely reception in their beautiful home in Minneapolis. I had someone make an ankle-length, white cotton eyelet dress for the wedding and after the wedding I dyed it aqua, shortened it, and wore it for summer parties.

I was working as a receptionist when I got married and it was pretty well understood at that time that the company wouldn't want someone obviously pregnant greeting the public. I disguised it well for seven months, putting on only 15 pounds during the nine months. I made a maternity outfit, but took most of my old skirts, cut out a hole for my belly, and tied the ends together with bias tape. I didn't like being fat or pregnant. I was not looking forward to life as a mother. If I had been born thirty years later I think I would have continued my education, become a journalist, maybe a foreign correspondent, and if I had wanted kids I would have had my ova implanted in someone else's body. Who knows what would have happened? Maybe I would have been killed during enemy fire. Maybe I would have been fired or disgraced. Maybe I would have defected and become the wife of a Russian commissar. Or, maybe I would have won a Pulitzer Prize.

Well, we'll never know because that was not an option. The Pill had not been discovered. Think how the Pill has changed women's lives, as well as world events. Women then were expected to stay home and raise children. Today I am amazed that I adapted as well as I did, considering my attitude at the time.

The first home Carl and Carrie Olson lived in was turned into a machinery shop after he built the big house on the hill. From left are Ethel, Grandma, Esther, Grandpa, twins Stanley and Cecil.

Carl Olson poses with two of his favorite horses.

The big barn housed the farm animals. The hay loft was a favorite place to play.

Two serious Swedish twins, Cecil and Stanley Olson, pose for the camera.

The elder Olson daughter, Ethel.

*Brother Walter Olson is surrounded by his twin brothers, standing, Parker and
Parnell, and seated, Cecil and Stanley.*

Ethel Olson, looking very regal in her twenties.

Axel and Esther Swedberg's wedding photo.

Grandpa Olson, l938, when he was visiting his son Elmer in Minneapolis.

Two-year-old Dolores and her proud parents, Esther and Cecil Olson.

Hjalmer and Parnell Olson with their nephew, Richard Swedberg.

Elmer Olson served in the United States Army during World War 1.

Getting together for dinner in 1955 are, from left, Karen Olson, Richard Swedberg, Bob Olson, Parnell Olson, Esther Swedberg, Eunice Swedberg and Gertrude Olson.

The Julius Pederson family: From left, Grandma , holding Mabel, Clara, Oscar, Martin, and Grandpa. In front, Arnold, Agnes and Albin.

Shy little cousins, Shirley and Dolores Olson.

LeRoy Olson is anxious to drive the tractor.

Gertrude Olson poses in front of their new car in 1941.

The car's the star as Parnell Olson shows it off.

LeRoy Olson, with a mouthful of sucker, poses for the camera with his big sister, Dolores.

That shy little first grader in the front row, right, is the author.

Grandma Esther and Grandpa Cecil Olson spend Christmas in South Bend with their daughter Dolores Liebeler, and four children, from left, John (Doc), Nancy, Carol, and baby JoAnne,.

It's the seventies! From left, Nancy, Mother (Dee), Carol and JoAnne Liebeler.

Chapter 8

After WWII

From one room overlooking the Mississippi River on the University campus I now had moved to one room in a basement apartment in South Minneapolis. It was our first home, and it was where our son John would spend the first year of his life. The kitchen side of the apartment held a card table and four chairs, a double hot plate, and orange crates piled atop one another served as cupboards. Mother gave me several green floral flour sacks which I made into curtains to cover the open crates. On the other side of the room was a double bed, an overstuffed chair and a small Duncan Phyfe mahogany end table which was a wedding gift. The bassinet sat at the end of our bed. I had a real playhouse with a real baby now. We had agreed that he would be christened John Raymond Jr., but it would be too confusing to call him by his father's name, and we didn't like Junior so we just called him *the baby* for a few days. Then, one day my husband looked at him and said, "What's up, Doc?" and Doc became his name. My husband had to drop out of school now that he had a wife and child to support. His plans for becoming a doctor had come to an end. He had transferred his dreams to his son.

There was an acute shortage of housing after World War II, plus a ceiling on rental property. Jack's high school buddy, Bob Ries, and his wife Lois were in the same boat we were—recently married and a baby, and no place to live. By sharing expenses and paying the landlord a $2500 bonus under the table, we were able to move into a two-bedroom first floor duplex near the campus. We got along well and had our dinners together for a short time, which would have been ideal except for the fact that Bob was really finicky. Too bad, because Lois and I were enjoying planning a menu and cooking together. Bob didn't like salads and the only vegetables he would eat were peas, corn and carrots. Mashed potatoes, if I sprinkled paprika on them, he'd dig around and under to find an untarnished glob. We took turns cleaning the house, and never had any disagreements, enjoying each other's company.

Lois had an easy laugh and a good sense of humor. One day a magazine salesman came to the door and we invited him in and listened to his pitch. He was not going to take no for an answer, just wouldn't leave. Finally, Lois brought out several pretty potholders her mother-in-law had made and offered the salesman a deal: "If you buy these, then I will buy a subscription." He left. No sale for him or her.

Lois and I relied on Dr. Spock's baby and child care book. Thirteen months later when my second child, Carol, was born, Spock's book was missing a cover, plus several pages. Lois was the "good mother" and breast-fed Steven, but I had already given up on that without giving it much of a try. I felt like a cow back on the farm when I tried it briefly and I did not like the idea of having to miss everything that was going on in the room by adjourning to my bedroom to feed my child. I was delighted to put him on a bottle. Lois and I spent our days washing diapers, changing diapers, cleaning house, fixing meals, and the extent of our social life was going to the in-laws for Sunday dinner. Occasionally I'd load the car with baby bottles, diapers, a diaper pail, a playpen, a bassinet, Gerber's baby food, and clothes and go 100 miles west to Willmar to see my folks for the weekend. I read a lot. I was shocked when I read Norman Mailer's' *The Naked and the Dead* in 1949. Fuck, fuck, fuck. Every other word! Certainly *no one* talked that way! But my husband, who had served in the Army Air Corps, said they did.

I tried to do what mothers were expected to do and actually knitted a sweater and cap for my son and a sweater and booties for Carol. I liked it better when they got older and I could show them how to paint, take them to museums, and read to them and tell them stories. We had Golden Books but they especially liked my dramatic "thump, thump, thump" when I read Edgar Allen Poe's "Tell Tale Heart." I made up stories about Fat Francis and Skinny Stanley, not realizing that I was probably setting them up for prejudice against fat people. Fat Francis would get stuck on the slide and Skinny Stanley could stand sideways and you couldn't see him!

Those days of child bearing and child rearing took us to different homes. We lived in Duluth, Minnesota for a year. We rented the first floor of a magnificent two-story brick home on Superior Street, where gated driveways and beautifully landscaped yards were commonplace. But, again, one huge bedroom for a family of four. A young IBM employee and the mother of our landlord, an 86-year-old woman, lived upstairs. She left the house each day, decked out in lots of jewelry, to play bridge. The basement apartment was occupied by a young woman, whom I never saw, but my husband reported that once when he went down to look at the furnace she flipped open her robe, and had nothing underneath. She had a lot of visitors. There were big cars parked outside our house all the time so she wasn't lonely.

We bought our first television, a seven-inch set that usually delivered very snowy pictures. I joined the Newcomers Club and we had couples over for bridge and went to their house. One of the bridge players brought out pizza that she had made. We had never heard the word, and it was like a pie crust with cheese and tomato sauce. Different, I thought, but I didn't ask for the recipe. Years later we would drive from South Bend to Chicago just to get Chicago's absolutely delicious Deep Dish Pizza.

Then, after only one enjoyable year in Duluth, Jack was transferred back to Minneapolis and we now rented a house near Lake Nokomis. Child No.3, Nancy, was born. By now I had settled into being a mother and was careless about using a diaphragm, actually welcoming another because the other two would soon be in school. The house was big enough for our family, and Jack and I finally had our own bedroom. We had just painted the bedroom walls burgundy and the dining room chartreuse—yes, the color of the year—when General Motors transferred him again, this time to Davenport, Iowa.

Like most mothers at that time, I experienced the joys and frustrations of raising children, but the need to write was still there. It was a time when contests were big. Tell why you liked a product in 25 words or less and you could win thousands of dollars. Kool-Aid ran a lot of contests and we always had that in the house so I entered those and won a TV and some small prizes. Then I won two cars, and I didn't know how to drive. Jack already had a company car so we sold the cars, paid bills, bought new living room furniture and took a ski trip to Aspen.

I know what won the Mercury Phaeton Hardtop which was given away on the Ed Sullivan TV show because I sent in numerous entries with different names, Mrs. J.R., Dee, Mrs. Jack—well you get the idea. Here it is:

Power and beauty in motion
With a picture window view
It's the Mercury Phaeton Hardtop

_____

The winner:
Sweet purring roadhug relaxes you.

Doesn't sound so great, does it? But I had researched the judging company and they liked original material, and the "roadhug" must have grabbed their attention because later I saw the Mercury on a billboard and it was called "The Road Hugger." It was advertised as having torsion air suspension, which Jack said made for a smoother ride.

The judging company did a good job of finding me. Although we were living in Davenport at the time, we were spending our vacation at a relative's cottage in Minnesota, where there was no phone. When no one answered the Davenport phone they checked with neighbors there and fortunately we had left our Minneapolis address with them. Then the guy called the Liebeler residence in Minneapolis, and got the telephone number of another lake resident who owned a phone. When the neighbor came running over to our cottage one day to tell us that someone needed to talk to me, I obviously thought it would be some very bad news. The contest investigator never divulged the nature of his call to anyone, and after I talked with him I had to meet with him to assure him I had written the entry.

I also sent in little stories to the *Reader's Digest* and won $25 for this true story: Some years back I had been trying to teach my 4-year-old son how to add. I held up one finger and then another and asked, "How many fingers do you see?" He looked at them, thought for few seconds, and said "two." Now I held up two fingers on each hand and again he thought and came up with the correct answer. Now I tried three fingers on each hand and he quickly snapped, "Six!" Amazed, I asked him how he was able to you figure that out so fast. "Because of Dad's six-pack of beer" he said. That should be a clue of what's to come some years later.

The first four years in our new home were typical of a suburban couple. We were like the neighbors, lots of young kids, having coffee together, mowing our lawn, planting trees. And having babies, including me with daughter No. 3, JoAnne. I was unhappy with Jack's drinking, staying out late, and gambling. Now I had four young kids, no college degree, so what could I do? He didn't want me to work and what money I could make from some menial job would barely cover child care, I knew. I just had to hope that things would get better and try to win a few more contests. We were deeply in debt. We had borrowed money from his folks and mine.

One Sunday when all I had for dinner was a 17-cent package of Kraft macaroni and cheese I knew I had to find a job. It was just before Christmas and I easily found work selling clothes at a nearby shopping center. It paid only $1.25 an hour, but it did put food on the table. I still had to hire a baby sitter for my youngest daughter who was in kindergarten during the morning.

We had a new tri-level home in a newly developed area in South Bend where a new elementary school had been built. I was elected the PTA president, and when the school celebrated its first year anniversary I wrote a skit. One of the board members worked at *The South Bend Tribune*. Their society editor had to have surgery, he said, and apparently he liked the skit I wrote and mentioned that there would be an opening at the paper. "Would you be interested in working there?" he asked. "I can't promise you the job, but if you're interested, I'll put in a good word for you." I told him I was definitely interested. I called personnel the next day. I had filled out a resume several months earlier. The personnel manager told me to come in for an interview and I was hired. That was the beginning of my career and the beginning of a new Dee. When the society editor came back I moved into the news department as a general assignment reporter, writing features stories, and then I became the editor of the youth section. When I left, I was the art critic, and also had the higher education and medical beats.

Things didn't get any better at home, but I knew as soon as I could support my children by myself I wouldn't put up with Jack's shenanigans any more. My kids and I saw their father come home drunk, staggering and yelling at them to go to bed at eight o' clock at night, seeing his car chained to a post where he had missed the corner, picking up the newspaper and seeing a picture of his car in a ditch, and standing at the door with a policeman after another accident. I had picked him up at the hospital and jail on other occasions. He spent nights away from home. I hated him. Then I'd feel sorry for this pathetic human being who could have accomplished so much. He was smart, handsome, articulate and sociable. I was afraid he had died in an auto accident when he didn't show up during the early morning hours. Then I'd get so angry I'd wish he was dead.

There were a lot of heavy drinkers in the newspaper business and I sat next to the business editor who attended AA each day. He suggested I go to Al-Anon and that was the best move I ever made. I didn't realize that I had been an enabler, making excuses for my husband, while preaching and nagging. *He's not feeling well today. He has the flu. He will be in later; he has a dental appointment this morning.*

When would I open the window and shout, "I'm not going to take it any more." We had been to a Press Club function on a Wednesday night and had a good time; he didn't drink too much for a change. We went home and made love, and I really though he was changing. He went to work the next day, but he didn't come home that night. Or Friday night. Or Saturday night. I called the Elkhart car dealership where he worked and he wasn't there. His boss seemed surprised at my call. Apparently Jack or someone had called in with some excuse. No word from my husband for three days! Then on Sunday afternoon one of his friends called and said Jack would be home for dinner that night. I couldn't believe such gall. He couldn't call me himself. He had to have a buddy do it. I had had it. I was done with this marriage. No forgiving this time. *And he thinks I'm going to fix dinner for him!?* That was it. On Monday I saw an attorney.

I filed for divorce. My older children encouraged me to do so. I had hung to my marriage as long as I could. Why had I put up with his infidelity for so long? I kept thinking *he could change, stick together for the sake of the kids, where would I go, how could I take care of the children by myself.* He could still be so charming. I still loved him when I thought of all his good qualities. I knew I would miss the kisses and caresses and crumpled sheets.

Making the decision to get a divorce was the toughest thing I had ever done. But once I made the decision and the papers were filed I felt a relief. Not legally divorced, it was already over for me, period. And now I didn't hate him. I felt sorry for him. He suffered from low self esteem, I told myself. And I knew I wasn't helping that feeling because I was getting better and better at what I was doing. I was getting promoted, getting a lot of respect in the community for my work. I didn't feel as if I had failed him and caused him to be unfaithful, by any means, at any time. He had a disease that had affected the entire family. *So let's move on with your life, Dolores,* I said to myself.

A year earlier Jack had been having an affair with an attractive bridge player whom a lot of the male players knew very well, as well as Jack did, if you get what I mean. Her husband and Jack showed up at my house late one night to bring me into a discussion. Jack got me out of bed and I went down to the kitchen to listen to the story. I wasn't surprised at the news, but was surprised that the guy was going to file an alienation of affection suit. I listened, and in my typically calm Scandinavian way, I said I had to get up early and was going back to bed, which I did. I was subpoenaed to testify, but was never called because I would never give the lawyer any idea what I would say. A change of venue was granted and for three days I traveled to another city with my husband, and got paid for sitting around and reading a book. I couldn't believe the law suit, and figured it probably did nothing but enhance Jack's feelings about his sexual prowess. I wondered, did those other guys that she had been sleeping with feel lucky, or a little slighted. We certainly didn't have any money so I didn't know what the law suit was supposed to accomplish.

Shortly after the divorce was final Jack stopped by the house one Sunday afternoon to see if there was any mail. The kids were out, but I said they'd be home for dinner, so I invited him to stay. "Well," he said, "I can't. We're leaving for Florida. I'm moving there and I have someone waiting in the car."

I looked out the window and saw a woman in the car."Bring her in. You can't be in that much of a hurry to leave," I said, pointing out that the kids would certainly want to see him before he left the state.

She came in and Jack introduced her. She was all-right looking, rather plain, nothing striking about her. I offered them something to drink, specifying coffee, tea or a soft drink. They said coffee. In my typical reportorial fashion I asked them where they would be going, what she did, what he planned to do there, and so forth. They seemed uncomfortable so I guess I did most of the talking. She was a nurse. They were going to stay with Jack's folks who lived there at the time. And he was going to buy a car dealership. The kids arrived shortly and he did get a chance to say good bye to them.

Jack had signed a quit-claim deed, turning the house over to me. Now I had to make the $125 monthly payment myself. I was supposed to receive $40 a week child support for Nancy and JoAnne, the two under 18. However, as soon as he moved to Florida the checks arrived later and later, until he was months behind in child support. I knew that if I took legal action the lawyer was going to charge me. I had an idea: I took the letterhead from my lawyer's correspondence and copied it onto a blank sheet of paper and wrote a letter to me as if it was coming from the lawyer's office. Then I made a copy and sent it to Jack. It worked. I know, it was dishonest. I don't remember what I said, but I know I did not sign my attorney's name. I made it very brief and formal-looking, and probably used threatening words like *extradition* and *jail* in it.

Chapter 9

A Wonderful Jungle

That hard-working car salesman comes home late, staggering and boozy-breath, and Dee asks him why he is so late. She just doesn't understand how hard he has to work to make a sale. *It's a jungle out there.*

Now *I* was in that jungle. And no one told me that I'd meet interesting people, have lunch at a nice restaurant, get dressed up each day, lookin' good, having co-workers tell you what a fine job you are doing and what a ray of sunshine you are. Wow! All this and I got paid for it.

Oh, I still had to go home and make dinner for the kids, clean, wash and iron. But it was a lot easier these days. Only thirty years ago I had to use an outdoor toilet, light a kerosene lamp, hang clothes outdoors, or freeze because the fire went out in the furnace. Now I installed an air conditioner in the bedroom window and bought a dishwasher. All the kids were in school. I was the only mother on the block who worked. I did the den mother and Camp Fire leader bit—enjoyed doing crafts with the kids a lot—and got involved in school activities. I liked baking, so the cookie jar was usually full—sometimes with Oreos, which the kids seemed to like better than my homemade chocolate chip or peanut butter cookies. The menu didn't vary much from week to week: spaghetti, hamburger and cheese on English muffins, pigs in blankets (sausages wrapped in Bisquick dough), fried chicken, five-can casserole (tuna fish mixed with soups and topped with crunchy chow mein noodles), macaroni and cheese, a tomato soup, macaroni and hamburger casserole, and on Sunday, either a beef or pork roast or chicken and dumplings.

There is no doubt that if I had been able to stay home and keep a closer eye on my kids we wouldn't have had as many crises. But you do what you have to do to survive and survival meant paying the rent and feeding and clothing my family. Indiana University had a South Bend campus and with the older children holding part-time jobs and some help from me they were able to enroll. Nan got a full scholarship to Indiana University in Bloomington, which, when she was informed of it, said, "Well, I guess I'll go to college then." Up to that point, she really had no interest in going to college.

I didn't plan to talk a lot about my kids in this book, but I think this is a story worth telling: It was Nan's senior year and I had dropped her off at John Adams High School every morning on my way to work. Our local deadline was noon. At about 11 a.m. my phone rang and it was the high school nurse. "Mrs.Liebeler?"

"Yes," I said.

"Nancy will need an excuse from the doctor after a two-week absence from school."

"What? There has to be some mistake!"

No, Nancy hadn't had pneumonia. I had dropped her off at school each day. However, the nurse soon convinced me it was my Nancy. Oh my God. What should I do? I called home. Nancy answered, and as calmly as I could I asked her why she was home. She said she was sick and came home. I said I would be home for lunch and see her soon. I felt numb as I drove through the streets, trying to figure out what had been going on, and what would I say to her? I imagined all kinds of things. *She had a boyfriend and was seeing him during the day. She was using drugs. She was selling drugs.* As the editor of the youth section I was aware of what was going on.

She was upstairs in bed, reading. I told her about the call from the nurse. She said, "Mom, I just turned around and walked home after you dropped me off. I couldn't stand going into that classroom." We both cried. We talked for a long time about finding a job and quitting school, about not graduating with all of her friends. I convinced her that we better go to the school and talk to the principal. She did want to graduate with her class but she also wanted to find a job.

The principal listened to her and empathized with her. It was the early '70s, the time of the hippie culture, when values were changing, when people were demonstrating their opposition to the Viet Nam war and nuclear weapons. It was difficult to keep a class under control, he admitted. He could understand why she was bored. He wisely told her she could look for a job, but if she didn't find one she could work with children who were in a special education class in the afternoon and take the courses she needed for graduation in the morning. She accepted his offer and went back to school the next day.

It turned out to be a life-changing event. She would think of projects for the children at night and bake a cake when someone had a birthday. Her life had a new purpose. She was more than just the peace-keeper in the family now. Four years later she graduated from the university with honors, majoring in special education. I am so grateful to that principal who listened, and understood.

The woman with the byline Dolores Liebeler met some interesting people while working in that wonderful newsroom jungle. I was able to take part in transactional study group conducted by Dr. Thomas Harris, the author of *I'm O.K. You're O.K.* Dr Harris said each person is the sum of three persons: parent, adult and child. He offered this example: The husband misplaces his cuff links. He asks his wife if she has seen them. The parent in you might say, "If you put them in the same place each time, you wouldn't have to look for them." The adult: "I'll look. I'll help you find them." The child: "I didn't take them." That is a simplified version but it did reveal behavior, and hopefully direct it in a more positive way. Keeping *that child within us* as an adult was important to our happiness, he said.

William Buckley was pompous and sneering, but quotable. Jane Fonda addressed Notre Dame students and there were older people in the front row who showed their displeasure with her Viet Nam action by throwing eggs at her.

Because of a mix-up I ended up in a limousine during a motorcade through the city when Sargent Shriver was running for vice president in 1972. I was supposed to interview his wife Eunice, who was supposed to ride in the third limo from the front, but she apparently didn't get the word and got into the second car with her husband. I was in the third limo when the cars started to move. People lined the streets and began waving. I'm in the back seat, alone. *People will wonder who I am. They probably think I am someone from the Kennedy family.* So I started waving and smiling a very toothy smile, trying to look like a Kennedy.

My editor was counting on a story from me. The best I could do, I thought, was relate what was happening, and interview the two Secret Servicemen in the front seat. Their first names were Harry and Sam. But when I pressed for more information, Sam said, "We can't talk. Regulations, you know."

However, I continued with innocuous questions. I had to have *some* kind of a story. I explained what my assignment was and they said they would make a last ditch effort to get Mrs. Shriver for me before the plane took off. We reached the airport, and Mrs. Shriver apologized for the mix-up and said she could give me a few minutes for an interview. I began asking her some questions as she took her typically long strides across the tarmac. But the noise of the plane was drowning out most of the answers. I heard her charge the Nixon administration with "corruption and indifference to humanity," then missed statistics and figures and who knows what else as the engine roared in my ears. Sam or Harry moved in, said she had to leave. I went back to the office, wondering what I would write. All I could do was write about my crazy experience. It turned out to be a funny story. I was surprised when I saw the story made the front page the next day.

Then there was Edward Teller, the "Father of the Hydrogen Bomb." He was so paranoid, agreed to answer only two questions and they would have to be topics he wanted to discuss. He didn't like the press, "Your nefarious actions are unjustified," he told me.

I rode in the station wagon with Paul Newman when he was campaigning for Kennedy and was offered a Coors beer as I interviewed him. I refused. There was Gail Sheehy, the author, and Wilfred Sheed, novelist and satirist. I felt better about being a working mom when he said our generation was obsessed with watching kids. "Having children does not require going into a 20-year monastic experience," he said. The Zen Buddhist Alan Watts said "the idea of God has worn thin because man looks at human life as no more than a pilgrimage from the maternity ward to the crematorium."

I don't remember all the celebrities I interviewed, but I loved every bit of it. Only Father Theodore Hesburgh, the president of the University of Notre Dame, terrified me. I was supposed to interview him on a local TV version of Meet the Press shortly after I started at the Trib. To prepare myself for the interview I went to the morgue (the paper's library), and read everything I could on Father Hesburgh and the university. I wrote down questions that I could ask. The show began and I had to ask the first question. I don't remember what it was, but Father Hesburgh looked at me and said, "That's a good question, Dolores." Then he went on and on for several minutes with his answer. There was someone else on the panel who asked another question, and by the time the half-hour was up, I think we had asked no more than four questions between us. In my years at the newspaper and my coverage of Notre Dame I regarded Father Hesburgh as a most magnificent human being—always a champion for students' rights, women's rights, and human rights. It was a privilege to have known him.

A few years later I would be known as the first woman in the Notre Dame Press Box. Another exclusive domain of the male had been invaded in a big way. On that day four St.Mary's College girls joined the Irish leprechauns' cheer-leading squad and seven women were issued tickets for the Notre Dame student section. The view from the press box was different—like watching the game on a giant TV screen. The cheers of the crowd were muffled, as if the sound had been "canned." Everyone was pretty quiet. There was an unwritten rule that you don't cheer or show partiality. Although a big deal was made of my being the first woman in the Notre Dame Press box, it wasn't true. Western Union women on the teletype machines had been a familiar sight to the press box for 20 years. They didn't count apparently because *they just worked there.*

It was the same way when I filed a sex discrimination suit in 1971 against the South Bend Press Club because they wouldn't allow women to attend their annual gridiron show. Who do you think had waited on the tables and served the men their dinner all those years? Again, those women didn't count. I sincerely thought I was just 'one of the guys' in the news room. As a member of the Press Club and their newsletter editor, I wanted to bring our club up to date. I had read what Gloria Steinem, Betty Friedan and Bella Abzug were doing and what was happening at the press clubs in New York, Chicago, Boston and other major cities. Helen Thomas, Washington Bureau chief from 1974 to 2000, a familiar figure in the front row of Presidential conferences, had already broken the barrier as early as 1962 when she was invited to the correspondent's dinner.

I sent in my check for the show, but it was returned. The show was not open to women, they explained. I contacted the Indiana Civil Rights Commission and filed a class action sex discrimination suit along with the other women on the paper. The case bounced in and out of the courts for three years—I won, they won, I appealed, they appealed—with the last decision favoring the club. The story made the *New York Times* and was headlines in *The South Bend Tribune*. I had found out the hard way that *men* make the decisions and *they* invite women to participate and women better not try entering a male bastion unless they are willing to make some enemies as well as friends. And put up with all the crap that comes from fighting for a cause. I was naïve about the action I took, never expecting such a furor. I thought it was something that should be done and I could do it.

However, politicians know that at least half their constituency is women, so with the announcement that the show would continue to be for men only an amazing thing happened: Several local politicians called the Press Club president and said they just couldn't attend the dinner if that was the policy. It was getting close to show time again and the guys directing the show were probably getting a little panicky. Well, they had won, they had been proven right, so they could now be gentlemen and invite us to the show. They made the big announcement the night of the dinner and asked the mayor's wife, who was seated at the table near the stage, to stand. Then they pointed out that several women from the news room were also attending. We were at a table toward the back of the room.

It made me a local leader in the women's movement. I gave speeches at men's organizations when they wanted to hear more about "those feminists." I was a bit apprehensive going into the Rotary Club or a Legion Hall, I admit. Maybe someone would throw eggs at me. They never did.

But that experience helped me make a lot of changes later in subtle and less painful ways. For example, when the Decathlon Athletic Club in Minneapolis wouldn't allow women to have lunch in the first floor dining room, I went in and joined my husband and his friends. When they said they couldn't serve me, I smiled and politely said, "That's all right. I won't eat." That caused more commotion. The waiter turned away and brought the manager to the table. Fortunately, my husband and his friends didn't think the policy was fair. Ron DeHarpporte was the first to speak up and question the waiter. Then the guys had fun, forcing the manager to explain *that women could always eat in the main dining room, that men often had to grab a quick lunch; men did business during lunch.* As long as I was at the table the five men at the table couldn't be served either, so, "Let's go," one of them said. We all got up, left the water and rolls at the table, and went someplace else. Love those guys! The club soon changed its policy.

The Decathlon also changed its policy when two women with very short hair complained that they had been kicked out of the pool because they weren't wearing bathing caps. They were furious because a man with much longer hair than theirs was allowed to stay in the pool. The Decathlon employee told the girls that he was just obeying the law: women had to wear bathing caps in the pool. I listened to what my friends told me and called the health department when I got home. There was no such law. I told the gals this and they took care of the matter immediately. They had more clout than I because both had husbands who were on the Decathlon Board.

A new woman was emerging in the '70s and I was one of them. Many, however, were opposed to my actions. During my Press Club law suit, there was a woman who frequently called me about 5 o'clock in the morning, calling me a stupid bitch and a lesbian, ranting and raving about my actions, then hanging up immediately after her tirade, apparently pleased that she had awakened me. I guess she had never flown because she screamed, "I suppose you want to use the men's bathrooms too." It's possible, had I known the stress it would cause and the relationships that it would damage, I may not have taken the action I did.

When I look back at the little farm girl who looked to my city cousin to come up with ideas, I try to figure out why I changed so much.

Maybe it's an innate Viking spirit, somewhat tamed and non violent, but still vain, proud and inquisitive. I realize I was hired for a "man's job" at a time when women of my generation were expected to stay home, take care of the house, their husband and their children.

Except for the religion editor, the receptionist and the women in the society department, I was the only female writer in the news room when I was hired. It was a large room with windows along one wall, functional, plain and crowded. It was a typical news room with typewriters, telephones, and paper on the desks—all lined up for more than 30 reporters, editors and associate editors, news and editorial writers. Wastebaskets rarely bulged with discarded words because deadlines inhibit perfection. Facts. Accuracy. That's what is important, and if the journalist has the creative ability to find that "hook" that takes the reader through the story he and paper are fortunate.

The *South Bend Tribune* was recognized as among the most advanced in the newspaper industry. When I left in 1973 I was typing my stories on a keyboard that sent signals to the computer—a large machine housed in an environmentally controlled room—where my story was set into a proper column widths, faces and sizes selected, and even words hyphenated where necessary. The men who made up the pages no longer stood over large metal plates to set the type. Now the composing room employees worked off a "dummy sheet" which was a miniature layout of the page, then a camera shot a full-page negative of the paste-up. When I was hired we plugged in fans to keep cool during the summer. When I left, there also were six other women on the news staff and we had air conditioning. I didn't need paperweights any more to keep my papers from flying off the desk.

At 83 I look back and I can see how women have advanced over the years. For me it has taken almost forty years. I am lucky to have been active in and a part of that revolution.

I look at "Rules of Conduct for Teachers" issued by the Board of Education, Cabell County, West Virginia, in 1915, and I can hardly believe them. I cite just a few:

> *"You will not marry during the term on your contract. You are not to keep company with men. You must be home between the hours of 8 p.m. and 6 a.m. unless attending a school function. You may not loiter downtown in ice*

> *cream stores. You may not dress in bright colors. You may,*
> *under no circumstances, dye your hair. You must wear*
> *two petticoats. Your dresses must not be any shorter than*
> *2" above the ankle."*

And, of course, they were expected to keep the schoolroom neat and clean, sweep the floor, start the fire at 7 a.m. so the room would be warm by 8 o'clock when school started.

So, how far have we come in less than one hundred years? Now, nearly a quarter million women have served in Iraq and Afghanistan, but we still have no ERA, as Ellen Goodman, retired columnist for the *Boston Globe* pointed out. She also noted that half the law and medical students today are female. But only fifteen of the Fortune 500 companies have female CEOs. We did have Hillary Clinton make a most serious run for the White House and a mother of five and a governor of Alaska made a run for the vice president. However, Goodman noted, women earn six out of 10 college degrees . . .yet earn 77 cents for every male dollar.

True, a woman is now the speaker of the house and at 60, Meryl Streep played a romantic lead in a movie, but "girdles have been resurrected as body shapers and girls are forced into ever-more narrow standards of beauty," said Goodman.

Progress. I hope to live long enough to see a woman as the President of the United States.

Chapter 10

Back to Minnesota

Bridge and work held me together when my marriage was falling apart. I looked forward to Friday night and duplicate bridge at the South Bend YMCA. After the game we would go to someone's house, sometimes mine, and have pizza and a few drinks, and discuss the hands for hours. My steady partner, Juhne, and I were hooked on the game and started to play in tournaments. Her husband had a plane and Friday was my day off. He would fly us to out-of-town tournaments for the weekend, then pick us up Sunday afternoon so I could go back to work on Monday.

We didn't know it at the time, but Tom, Juhne's husband, was so willing to fly us to tournaments because then he could fly to Colorado to see his girlfriend. He was ultimately shot to death in his bed by the Colorado woman's other lover. Now there was a juicy story for the *South Bend Tribune* readers! And, sadly, a very painful experience for my dear friend who had six young children.

Juhne and I arrived in Milwaukee one Friday and were about to register for the side game when a tall, heavy-set man tapped my friend on the back. Juhne stood out in a crowd like Marilyn Monroe, a little plump but curvaceous, white hair, big blue eyes, and she knew how to dress: high heels on shapely legs and expensive clothes that accented her curves.

"Honey, you don't want to play in a side game. I need a partner in the mixed pairs event, how about it?" the stranger said. She looked up at him with a shocked expression and said, "I'd *never* leave my friend!"

"Okay, okay, hold on a minute, don't buy an entry, I'll be right back," he said, turning around quickly, running toward the door.

Before we had time to discuss what we should do, he returned with a guy wearing a summer seersucker jacket in September and a tie that wasn't knotted but flipped over like an ascot. But it was too narrow for an ascot. And his striped shirt and tie didn't go well together. He was lean and nice looking though, seemed pleasant, and both Juhne and I preferred to play in the main event, rather than a side game.

Don Horwitz and I sat down and filled out a convention card, and I noticed that he was a Life Master, and I thought to myself, why is he going to play with me, a beginner? There had been some romantic liaisons at our local club that began when the beginning player was taken under the wing of a better player. And into bed, I should add. I was suspicious, but I'd show him who was boss at the table, I thought. The very first hand I bid aggressively and reached a small slam and went down one. (Contracting for 12 tricks, and taking 11) He pointed out how I could have made it with a strip-end play, but realized from my confused expression that I didn't know what he was talking about, stopped his critique, shrugged his shoulders and said, "Well, that's yesterday's newspaper." He never forgot the hand, and loved to tell the story years and years later, naming all the cards I held. *And if she throws him in with a diamond East has to lead a heart back. . .*

That was eerie: *That's yesterday's newspaper.* He didn't know I was a reporter. We managed to "scratch" (win some points) and so did Juhne and her partner. It was the beginning of a romance, and five years later, as soon as Don's divorce was final, we were married by the Justice of Peace in South Bend with all my children present. My friend Ren, who directed an Episcopal choir, sang something very classical, and my friend Bill, who had one of the best voices in the Press Club's Hoaxes show, sang "Because." The Judge's chambers were crowded with a couple dozen friends and family. It was 1972, the polyester and big hair era. Always one to attempt to adhere to the latest styles, I wore a long black and while polyester skirt and blouse and my bouffant hairdo was back-combed enough to hide a hornet's nest.

It was December and Don's drawn-out and contentious divorce finally went through. We needed to get married that month because of the "tax advantage," he said. A few weeks later I sold my house and moved to Minnesota. Don worked for the United States Bedding Co., a business his grandfather started in 1898 and headquartered in St. Paul. We moved into a two bedroom apartment in suburban Bloomington with my 13-year-old daughter, JoAnne. Jo thought Don was great—until we took her away from her home and her friends and moved her into that apartment. However, Don had an amazing amount of patience, eventually won her over, and became the father she needed in her life. Giving up my job as a reporter wasn't easy. I loved the job. I was well known in South Bend and my kids were proud of their mom. I had already turned down the opportunity to work full-time for the *Chicago Sun Times* because it would have meant moving my children to Chicago. But I thought I could work for a Minneapolis paper and I knew Don could offer me and my children the financial security that every woman wants. I wasn't madly in love with him, but he was loving, witty, intelligent, fun, thoughtful, and nice to my kids. What was best for my children, and me? I asked. I knew I needed to rule with my head and not my heart.

When I met his 86-year-old Jewish father, he was living alone in an apartment in St. Paul. I was a *shiksa* with big hair, and the height of current fashion in my mini-skirt. Lou Horwitz, always a gentleman, asked me to sit down, and offered me a drink. I said I'd have a scotch and water and he raised his eyebrows, then went to an interesting piece of furniture that opened up to a little bar and fixed two scotch and waters. He liked scotch, too, he said. Then he began to question me. Where was I from? Do you have family? What did I do? When he asked me where I grew up, I said, "On a farm." With an incredulous nod, a broad smile and a low chuckle, he said, "You sure don't look like a farm girl!"

As a child I grew up attending the Lutheran Church, the only church in town. Later, during my married life, I went to the Catholic, Episcopal, Methodist, Congregational and Evangelical Covenant churches on occasion, but never found answers, only declarations from the pulpit that their church was the best. I knew very little about Judaism, but religion never entered the picture with Donald and me.

It wasn't an issue, probably because we weren't going to have children. We both were in our mid-forties.

Typical of a college freshman, I had long ago tried to find "the meaning of life." I now was content to settle for Alfred Lord Tennyson's poem, "Flower in the Crannied Wall," that we had studied in English 101.

> *"Flower in the crannied wall,*
> *I pluck you out of the crannies,*
> *I hold you here, root and all, in my hand,*
> *Little Flower--but if I could understand*
> *What you are, root and all, and all in all,*
> *I should know what God and man is."*

His family and friends welcomed me warmly and enthusiastically. Not much of a challenge, I found out: his ex didn't care for his family and the feeling was mutual.

Several years into our marriage I decided to take a class to learn more about Judaism. I wanted to be able to hold a proper Seder, and know why the day was a special one for Jews. I wanted to set a table beautifully, serve the symbolic dishes and say the blessings so that Don and I could hold a Seder. During the three months of classes I learned a lot about Judaism. And we did celebrate Passover, usually with Christian friends because his children would celebrate with their mother. After we left Minneapolis, it was sometimes just the two of us, but we made the day a special one. Don was great in presenting a condensed version of the Passover Haggadah so I never had to worry about the food getting cold. He briefly explained the *matzo*, the unleavened bread; the *charoset*, an apple-nut-wine combination, the parsley dipped in salted water, the egg and lamb shank. All of us at the table would take turns reading portions of the Haggadah, and Don would, thankfully, skip portions so that it wasn't one of those Passover dinners that lasted for three hours. It did, however, give our guests some idea of the Seder ritual.

Although I enrolled in the classes so that I could participate more in family activities I discovered that Reform Judaism was what I had been looking for in religion. It allowed me to think, it didn't have definite affirmations about heaven or hell or who or what God is. I was impressed that Rabbi Lerner never put down any other religion and never tried to convert me. Nor did Donald ask me to convert. I had finally found my soul.

I am grateful that my parents weren't religious and gave me the chance to explore different beliefs. I think it is a shame how we automatically label children with our parent's religion. As a kid I got the heaven and hell pitch from an aunt but it seems terribly arrogant to me to think that we should expect more than we have on earth.

Science has proven that life evolved slowly and steadily, with natural selection the sculptor of life. The problem is not religion, per se, it's man. And I don't use *man* to encompass all humanity, because I can't think of any woman who has abused the faith the way, for example, Jim Jones did. More than 900 people believed, without questioning, and stupidly followed Jim Jones to Guyana and to their death when Jones laced Kool-Aid with cyanide. Or, more recently, why wouldn't the three who died after Arthur Ray's sweat tent 'cleansing' ceremony in Sedona question the practice and leave when they felt ill?

"Don't believe everything you hear," said Dr. Dee Anna Glaser, professor of dermatology at St. Louis University, who has studied the benefits of spending time in a sauna or spa or other places that make you sweat." There really are no medical benefits," she said, adding that the liver and kidneys do such a good job of ridding the body of toxins that there's almost nothing left for the sweat glands to purge.

She pointed out that people find it relaxing and that's not a bad thing, "but there isn't any specific health benefit."

I got expelled from a Life Spring seminar because I kept questioning the director. If something doesn't make sense and doesn't have some scientific basis, speak up, get out! The point of Life Spring seemed to be that "we alone are responsible for what happens to us." But when the young man sitting next to me was told that he had to take responsibility for his actions when someone had broken into his apartment and stolen several things, I had a few questions of my own. The man had locked his door. Ah, you don't question the director I found out. I was ordered to "Sit down" or "Stand up" whenever I had a question. At one point he removed my chair when I stood up. So I sat on the floor. After a couple days, I decided to quit. The director obviously didn't like my disruptions, and I couldn't stand his rationale. A representative did show up at my house the next day and asked me to return, but I said no, but wanted my money back for the remaining sessions. And I got it. No one, absolutely no one, questioned the leader's logic, so I did wonder what was wrong with me. Several months later I had an opportunity to ask a psychiatrist I met at a party about my actions and he congratulated me for not just following the leader. No danger in that. That happens to be the way I am.

It scares me today how Wahabi Muslim clerics have bastardized Islam and are preaching hatred and death to all who don't believe as they do. Again, it's follow the leader, no matter how insane they might be. But the same hatred comes from many of our religious leaders and ultra-conservatives who have no tolerance toward those who are gay and lesbian. I believe women, who have to carry a child for nine months, should be the ones to enter the pro choice-anti abortion debate, not men! Man's control over woman just doesn't stop.

There seems to be a fascination with psychic phenomenon today. Plenty of people are tuned in and ready to spend a lot of money for psychic readings. (A woman in West Bloomfield, Michigan is booked three years in advance for readings at $500 an hour.) Even though I don't believe in the ability to get in touch with the dead, nor do I believe in ghosts, I certainly find it entertaining. "It's all verbal tricks and mirrors," says magician James Randi, who has traveled the world as the Amazing Randi. During times of economic difficulty and uncertainty, interest in the supernatural skyrockets, according to an author of media and supernatural stories for teenagers.

Don and I had been married for only a few years when he found out that his kidneys were failing and he would need a transplant or eventually have to go on dialysis. Fortunately, he never had to go on dialysis because his son Tommy gave him one of his kidneys. That was quite a day: Don had his transplant in the morning and that evening I received a B.A. degree from Metropolitan State University, more than 40 years after leaving the University of Minnesota and getting married, raising four children and having a career as a reporter and editor. I now had another career. I was still writing, but for Honeywell.

My journalism skills served me well and I enjoyed the opportunity to use my creativity in advertising and marketing projects. I wrote speeches for the executives, created video tape and film scripts for in-house programs, and edited and wrote a lot of the annual report. The word had gotten out that I was a "feminist" so I ended up examining and changing a lot of the literature that had been for men only. For example, the old brochures said top Honeywell *salesmen* would be awarded an annual trip and their *wives* would be given an allowance for baby sitting or clothes. Well, times were changing. Women were selling and men were coming out of the closet. When one of the sales winners wanted to bring his gay partner on the trip, management realized it had to face a new problem. I was constantly re-wording our literature to make sure the company wasn't discriminating. About a dozen women were selected by the Honeywell President E.W. Spencer to start a women's task force to look into some of the specific problems that women faced in the workplace. I was one of those selected, and although I left the company in 1983 the task force (later called the Honeywell Women's Council) continued and was given corporate funding to sustain its efforts.

After less than a year in the Bloomington apartment we decided to look for a house. JoAnne obviously was not happy. She was sullen and difficult, and we didn't like her choice of friends. Don suggested that *she* pick out a school and a house. She said she wanted to go to Edina High School. It had a good reputation. We looked for homes in the area and then we'd take her there on Sunday. With most of the homes, she just walked in and turned around just as fast. Don was so patient. She finally approved of one that we could afford. "It's fine," she declared, without any expression. She was such a brat, but she had already let me know that I had taken her away from her friends, and, to make matters worse, she had just made the cheerleading squad when we moved.

The years in Edina went fast. I was working all the time. We had a lake cottage that we went to on weekends in the summer. We had many activities with our combined families. As Don's kidney began to fail, he became increasingly tired and he still suffered chest pains. Nevertheless, we managed to take a couple trips to Europe, a Mediterranean cruise, and played tennis on a regular basis. His company was sold, his health was deteriorating, and his chest pains were exacerbated by the cold weather. We had already looked into retirement homes in Florida, but it was while I was on a business trip to Scottsdale when he found the house we moved into a few years later.

Don got through the transplant, back surgery, a triple bypass, numerous TIAs, pneumonia, shingles and seizures. He survived several falls, high blood pressure, angina, skin cancer, and third degree burns after stupidly starting a fire with gasoline. Nothing stopped him. He went to a bridge tournament, his face all swathed in gauze. He went to a wedding a week after back surgery

Chapter 11

Early Retirement

Retiring wasn't an easy decision. I enjoyed working, but Don's health was getting worse and he wanted to move to a warmer climate. I worked for Honeywell for three years after he retired from King Koil because I wanted to become vested and receive some retirement benefits.

During those three years he learned how to use a wok because he wanted to have dinner ready for me when I came home from work. He had become so proficient in the art of wok cooking that he could fix almost anything on a Chinese menu. Forever confident, he decided to invite our kids—three couples in the cities at that time—to a Sunday Chinese dinner.

He had an office in the basement and when that Sunday came he went down there early that afternoon. The kids were coming at five o' clock. The refrigerator was filled with shrimp, beef and chicken, pea pods, broccoli, onions, carrots, celery, water chestnuts, and who knows what else. It was getting late. I thought I better remind him of the time because he hadn't started to chop up anything yet. He came upstairs a short time later, wearing a satisfied but impish expression, and handed me several menus which he had laboriously and painstakingly hand-printed with different colored pens. The kids could order by number, just as you do at a Chinese restaurant. No. l. Chicken and Pea Pods; No. 2. Kung Pao Chicken; No. 3. Chicken, bean sprouts and green onions; No. 4. Beef and broccoli; No. 5. Shrimp with pine nuts, and on and on—at least 10 different options. He had little comments underneath: "Dee's favorite," "Chef's specialty," and one was "Sold out."

The menus were a big hit. Everyone laughed. But the kids took him seriously. Or, they weren't going to let their Dad get by with this nonsense, so they studied the menus and put in their orders.

We chopped and stir-fried, and chopped some more. With only one wok and almost everyone ordering something different some just sat and waited while others ate. Hours later everyone was served and we were ready to join them, wisely deciding, "We'll have what she's having," loading up the wok with a triple batch of shrimp with pea pods. Finally, a very satisfied feeling took over as we joined our children at the table.

Donald never indulged in anything half-heartedly. When he was retired and before we moved to Scottsdale he renewed his interest in chess: He had two electronic chess boards going at the same time, reminding him in a monotone computer voice, "Your. Turn."

On a trip to Tucson he discovered the beauty of cactus while taking a tour through the desert. He was determined to take them home to the kids. Neither one of us knew that you couldn't just go out in the desert and just dig them up. We had dug up several small ones and one beautiful barrel cactus with yellow fruit. Don went to the grocery store and got cardboard boxes so that we could take them with us on the plane. His nephew Jamie, who was attending Arizona University, had given us his car to use and we picked him up the day we were to fly back to Minneapolis so he could take us to the airport. Jamie walked into our casita and saw us trying to pack up the cacti. The needles of the 12-inch barrel cactus kept popping through the sides. Now Jamie told us it was *illegal* to remove them from the desert. Okay, so we won't take them, I said, thinking that was settled. Donald was sure it would not be a problem and continued with the packing.

The smaller ones were neatly encased in a box, but the barrel's needles were popping out everywhere. It was Donald's favorite and he wasn't going to leave it there so he went and found a bigger box to hold that box, stuffing paper between the two boxes so the prickly needles wouldn't pop through. We got to the airport and I lagged behind, pretending I didn't know this man with two big boxes in his arms.

Don was right. No questions asked. They checked the boxes and they were on their way to Minneapolis. We gave the family cacti from

Arizona, and the barrel sat in our window in our Edina home for almost ten years. When we moved to Scottsdale we took the barrel cactus back to its Arizona home. It never bloomed in our window in Edina, but when we planted it in our yard in Arizona it grew and blossomed. We dug it up when we moved to a larger home, and it continued to grow. I peeked over the fence of our old house some time ago, long after we had downsized, and the little round barrel cactus was now over three feet tall, looking more and more like a small saguaro than a golden barrel.

Donald didn't know any strangers. He was fun, although sometimes an embarrassing travel companion. He talked to people on the elevator or airport shuttle and soon knew where they were from and where they were going and what they did.

We walked into a restaurant during Happy Hour and the place was packed, but Don saw a black couple sitting by themselves in a big booth and asked if they would mind if we joined them. They invited us to sit down with them we had a wonderful conversation. On more than one occasion I came home from bridge to find some strangers in my home—once in my bedroom. Don had been at Starbucks and joined a couple at a table and found out they were looking for a condo. He told them about our place and invited them to take a look at it because there were some for sale in our complex.

No one was photographed more often at his friend's wedding anniversary than he because he kept moving around, meeting everyone. Traveling with Donald was never dull. He led the way as we confidently boarded trains in Italy and France. But in the case of Italy, he thought we could buy a return ticket on the train and that's when we got in trouble because we didn't have a ticket and couldn't understand what the agent was saying. There was a big commotion, the agent was angry, waving his arms around. An American student came to our rescue. She explained that we didn't know better and we paid the fine. We framed the ticket when we got home.

When we were in London we walked into a discount store that sold china and crystal. Don saw the prices and thought we should buy a new set of china. So that is what we did. Ah, but here's the rub: We wouldn't be saving anything if we were going to have it shipped home so we decided to lug it around England and take it home on the plane with us. We schlepped around England for two weeks, carrying the bone china in the car, dragging it into a hotel each night. It was heavy, and the rope around the box would slip and come loose. If we carried it down the street for any distance Don would get chest pains and have to stop and rest. We managed to get it home and the only piece that broke was the gravy boat.

He loved a bargain, and always wanted to buy several if they were on sale. I should have realized that joining Costco was a big mistake. How long would it take for us to finish three big boxes of Cheerios? How long would it take to get through three giant-sized bottles of catsup? Did we really need that electric massage vibrator because it was on sale for only $89.95. Of course, we did, and it may have been used once or twice. Now we were living in a small condo, without a garage, so where would I store 48 rolls of toilet paper?

I don't like complainers and find ways to make things fun. Traveling down the freeway to go to work could be slow and require a lot of patience. I invented a game. If I couldn't make a word out of the letters on the car license plate in front of me I couldn't pass it. Sometimes I ended up late for work because the car in front of me had an impossible combination of letters, like XUK! We played it as a family, too, and the one with the shortest word was the winner. Years later when I remarried, Donald would play the game with me too. One day he said, "Oh, I got your new license plates today. *Well, that was certainly nice of him.* Knowing that I would quickly check to see what word I could make from the letters, I dashed into the garage to check out the plate. The letters were LOVEY. The vanity plate was a loving gesture. It was what he always called me, but it was often embarrassing. Horns would honk, people would stare and laugh, and I had a feeling someone might think I was advertising.

We met playing bridge and we continued as bridge partners throughout our married life. A lot of bridge players could point to us and issue this advice: "Don't play bridge with your spouse." Yeah, we argued about the game, but it was really the only thing we ever disagreed on. He was an excellent player, having won national acclaim, and I was his student . . . he thought. However, I am not the meek, mild and condescending type, so we'd argue about bids, and now that I had retired I had been reading bridge books and I had my own opinions. His memory of hands drove me crazy! He would never let go of a subject, no matter what.

Although he suffered from Alzheimers, he could still play a reasonable game. And I played with him at least once a week because it was what he loved to do. He had already been barred from the club on different occasions for his behavior and no one wanted to play with him. When the suspension was up we went back to the club and he kept his rage under control with me because he knew I wouldn't play with him if he got nasty. He also had been barred from playing bridge on the internet. He was playing bridge on the computer with some woman from Canada and she apparently made a really stupid mistake and Don, although a very slow hunt-and-peck typist, laboriously took the time to find the keys to write, "What the f...u...c...k do U think yre doin?" She reported him and he couldn't play for six months.

Taking care of an Alzheimer's patient is challenging. Don realized he had lost his mathematical skills, yet resented my control over the bills. Always generous, he now fussed about money constantly. Where our only arguments for more than 30 years had been about bridge, we now fought over many things. He thought he was still able to manage his affairs and take care of himself. I enrolled him in a senior day care center and that lasted a month. His mind was racing, he wanted to talk to people, he didn't want to engage in any of the activities. He repeated himself constantly, asking the same questions over and over, which is common characteristic of the disease. He refused to have someone come in to watch him for a few hours when he found out how much it would cost. He could threaten me one minute and call me Lovey and give me a hug the next.

Interestingly, what kept him busy and restored some confidence and kept him busy for several months was his searching for an assisted living home. He knew he was being consumed by the disease and felt, as Julie Christie did in the *Away From Her* movie, that he would be happier living away from me. That seemed to him the perfect solution.

There was no way that he could have lived there by himself, but I humored him because he was now happy that he had a solution. The Alzheimers seminars had helped me deal with him. *Just accept what the patient says, don't argue about it or tell them they are wrong.* Donald now was a little easier to live with. There were fewer arguments. He now had control of an issue. He would be busy on the computer, finding out about homes, talking on the phone with people. He was most encouraged by one woman who told him over the phone, "You don't sound like you have Alzheimers." It was what he wanted to hear; he was convinced he could make his own decisions.

We visited various assisted living homes, finally settling on one near the VA hospital because "then I can drive my scooter there when I need to see the doctors." (The VA was a couple miles from the home and not in a good part of Phoenix.) Typical of his gregarious nature, he would simply walk into a patient's room and start talking while we were on a guided tour of a facility. He was excited to show my daughters the home when they came to visit us. He surveyed the items he wanted to take to his new home: his dresser, the computer, and one of the beds. He couldn't walk for any distance without getting chest pains, and he dragged his feet. He had fallen several times, and ended up in the hospital. He had failed his driver's test. He had lost his bridge partners because of his behavior. He didn't think about eating. If he turned on the stove he'd forget to turn it off. He had to be bribed to take a shower. ('Honey, you get nice and clean and we can get in bed and cuddle' worked.) Even when Alzheimer's changed his personality and he became angry and mistrusting and wanted to get a divorce, he could quickly forget what he was angry about and hug me.

The hardest part about living with someone with Alzheimers is watching the slow irrational decline of their mind. I was used to taking hydrogen peroxide to remove the blood on his clothes and carpet because he bled so easily—just a slight bump and he would bleed. I often discarded his underwear rather than attempting to get them clean. He wouldn't consider wearing disposables.

During the last few years when he needed to be watched I spent a lot of time painting Christmas cards, acrylic and oil paintings from composites of photographs that I or someone else had taken. I'm sure most people didn't realize they had received an original 'Gavriella,' my Hebrew name, the one I used on my cards. If they tossed them away that was okay, it was a way to keep busy, something to do while staying home and taking care of Donald. But a lot of my friends have framed them and look forward to another one.

Bridge was Don's passion. He was 81. It was December 22, 2007, our 34th wedding anniversary, and we were looking forward to playing bridge at the local club and then going out to dinner. I had gone to have my hair done, and someone was at the house helping him with the computer. When I returned to pick him up for bridge, he was at the computer and he said he had fallen. He said the geek looked at it (his ankle) and everything was okay. I looked at the floor around the chair at the beige carpeting and it was red. There was blood all over, from the den to the kitchen. His ankle, his socks, his pant-leg and shoes were covered with blood. I didn't know where the cut was. I told him to take down his pants, and there on his left hip was a v-shaped gash, six inches up one side, four inches on the other. I grabbed a towel and wrapped it around the wound and took him to the emergency room. He got pneumonia, and died three weeks later. According to the woman who was at the house at the time, Donald went into the kitchen to answer the phone and fell against the coffee table in the living room, but got up right away. He examined his ankle, and so did she. Everything seemed okay, so she left, knowing I would be home shortly.

Chapter 12

Alone

My house was quiet after January 10, 2007. I used to hate the fact that Donald talked all the time. Now I didn't like the quiet. I turned on the radio or TV as soon as I got up, not paying much attention to what was being said. The quiet seemed ominous and foreboding.

Nancy, my middle daughter, and I were enjoying Happy Hour at a restaurant on Lake Minnetonka in Minnesota the summer after he had died when she asked about the stories Donald used to tell about his family. I remembered some of them. She thought I should write a book about the family. Hmm, I sipped my martini and agreed, it sounded like a good idea. After all, I love research and have been a writer all my life. It would be good therapy. I could do something Donald had wanted to do. And, I thought, it would be a wonderful gift for his family. I knew I would dedicate it to his memory.

Although I was 80 years old, I started to research, interview and write *Who Made My Bed?* with the help of Donald's cousin, Edward Bronstien, former president of the United States Bedding Co. Two years later it was done and we submitted it to a publisher. (We self-published. At 80 you don't spend the next 10 years looking for someone to publish a family story!) When I started writing the book about the men in the family's bedding business the title that immediately came to my mind was "Bedfellows." But that got a thumbs down from my co-author, apparently from what it could suggest. The book was almost done and

Edward and I still hadn't agreed on a title. The title came to us during a brainstorming session my daughter Nan and I were having on a return trip from the Grand Canyon. *Voila*! We had it: *Who Made My Bed?* The manuscript was ready to send to the publishers and we finally had a name that seemed right for the book. Edward loved it.

I felt fortunate after Donald died that I had a lot of interests: writing, reading, painting and bridge. I realized I knew very little about my family and decided to meet cousins I had never met and work on a book about the Olson family while I was working with the publisher on his family's book. I'm not very computer savvy. Consequently, it probably took much longer than it should have to get the book published.

* * * * *

Looking back, I knew that it was time for Donald to die when he did. People mean well when they try to console someone after death , but the *he's in a better place now* was offensive. I didn't respond, but I wish they had just offered their sympathy, given me a hug, said something nice about him. Six-feet-under is *not* a better place, but he wanted to be buried in Mt. Zion Cemetery in St. Paul, next to his mother, father and brother. Cremation is my option upon my death. Spread my ashes across some land, where the wind can carry me off like the white tufts left by golden dandelions. The small box of ashes after cremation—about the size of a shoebox—resembles bone-meal, the product that nourished my roses. Will my ashes assist the growth of nature? I have no idea, but it makes more sense than heaven or hell. I have respect for tradition, what others believe, and what can be defined as spiritual or close to God things. That golden field of dandelions is reality, far more beautiful than anything I could imagine, but it, too, will disappear in the wind, carrying its origin, leaving only slender stalks—a reminder of what it was: our memories.

I dislike the sanctimonious attitude that this—no matter what the belief—is the "only religion that is right." Asserting the superiority of one's beliefs is judgmental, offensive, and certainly bad manners. We can easily become victims of xenophobia or religious prejudice when we discriminate by differences, whether appearance or belief. There is nothing wrong with having a healthy skepticism toward authority and there's no law against proselytizing, but be wary that it isn't "brainwashing." There are many examples of religion going bad.

The fanatical teachings of Islam repress individual liberty and social equality, especially toward women. It is completely intolerant of the beliefs different from their own. The Wahabi sect of Islam, which directs Saudi Arabia's state religion, loathes Christians, Jews, other Muslims, women, anything modern and even freedom itself. It criticizes, and will not tolerate criticism. These are not the teachings in the Koran, but clerics have interpreted the writings to suit their own agenda: destruction of all who do not believe as they do. Now that is damned scary. But are the one-sided views of Christian Fundamentalism much different? They aren't preaching extermination of everyone else, but their belief is based on stories written by a number of men and not on science.

There is no area more repulsive and disgusting than the Vatican's attitude toward child molestation. The victims are the boys and girls who have been sexually assaulted by priests, nuns and seminarians for generations. Here is my cryptic suggestion: Have one of the world famous Nevada brothels establish a satellite business inside the Vatican so the priests can leave the children alone. And then someone can write a musical and call it, "The Best Little Whorehouse in Italy."

According to a 2010 Pew Forum on Religion and Public Life report, 18-29 year-olds are shunning traditional religious denominations but their faith in God appears nearly as strong as that of earlier generations. The report says roughly three-quarters of Americans believe in an afterlife, and both non-believers and believers have increased. The study points out that participation in religious activities and belief in God tend to increase with age.

Only science can reveal the true greatness of this world. As yet I haven't seen any proof of the rewards in the 'Hereafter' being any better than the ones we have on this universe. The 'everlasting life' concept, on the other hand, deserves some study. Aren't we just a bunch of atoms bouncing off each other like billiard balls? Could we be as immortal as the sponge cell? I'll leave that to anthropologists and also listen to those who speak more ethereally and spiritually about our soul and our brain. As we learn more through genetic testing and DNA, we will learn more about our bodies and find better ways to treat diseases and ailments. Think about it, gene testing was originally aimed at finding the risk factors for cancer, diabetes and Alzheimers, and now it can reveal stuttering, compulsive leg-jiggling, and possibly determine the diet that works for people.

I'd like to learn more about our *soul*—an interesting word. Webster's defines soul as "the principle of life, feeling, thought, and action in man, regarded as a distinct entity separate from the body; the spiritual part of man as distinct from the physical part." We know what it is. And we don't know what it is.

Ayn Rand wrote that "man's own happiness is the moral purpose of life, with productive achievement his noblest activity, and reason, his only absolute." Our founding fathers didn't care if you were Protestant, Catholic, Jewish, atheist or even a follower of Mohammad as long as you observed the Constitution. Ben Franklin claimed he was a member of every church and prayed at all of them. The Dalai Lama says that for man to be happy he must make others happy. The goal of 60 Minutes—that highly successful TV show—is to tell a story. As Don Hewitt, their producer said, "Isn't that what the Bible is all about?

For those who have been labeled—not necessarily indoctrinated--with their parents' religion, faith may undermine science. But it certainly is easier to "just believe," to have actions that have been catalogued as good or bad or black or white by our religious doctrine. It is comfortable to "know the answers," and to avoid using our intellect to question the dogma. Is there a gray area? Should I believe the Bible 100 percent? If you do, that's faith. However, that attitude has never been a comfort to my questioning mind. Frankly, I don't take religion seriously. Think about it, if we are to take the seventh day as a day of rest, then what should we do if we see our neighbor mowing his lawn on Sunday. Go out and kill him? By now you know I like to say preposterous things. And then I'm surprised when someone takes me seriously.

What works for others is fine with me as long as it doesn't trample someone else's rights, or teach intolerance of other human beings, no matter what their religion, or lack thereof.

Chapter 13

Looking Back at 80 Years

This is remarkable. Where did the years go? Two husbands, four children and two careers seem to comprise my life. And I still feel young, and I'm healthy, a little arthritis, and that's about it. Thank goodness for those good Scandinavian genes.

Like the Miss America contestant who wants "peace in the world" mothers say their greatest pride is *their children*. Even my kids say I'm not an "ordinary" mom, but I won't dispute the popular and familiar response. However, back before birth control pills, the biggest problem was *not* having children. I think of Grandma and Grandpa Olson, that lusty, sexy couple who had a child almost every year for the first nine years of their married life. The method of birth control, pulling out before ejaculation, didn't work very well. The primary method of preventing pregnancy in those days was early withdrawal and douching. Early condoms were made of linen, silk or animal intestines. Grandma got a bit of a break after the first set of twins. We know her health deteriorated and Grandpa may have heeded her "not tonight." Maybe she finally got the old man to remember condoms when he drove that Packard into town.

Things didn't seem to be much better in 1948 when I got married. Our son was born a year after we were married and 13 months later, my daughter Carol. Now I needed to know what was causing all this and although I had a diaphragm and Jack often used condoms, I now decided we better use both at the same time. I also took my temperature to find out when I ovulated. I could curse those fertile Olson genes!

With two children just 13 months apart I was busy attending to their needs all the time, it seemed. How, I ask now, could Grandma Olson have managed with one child after another, year after year, and then two sets of twins? If some of the Olson boys were deprived of attention when they were little, I can understand why.

Once I became a mother and was comfortably settled in my own home, thoughts of being something more than a wife and mother disappeared. I actually enjoyed the lifestyle. Living in a neighborhood with many young mothers, I had a built-in support system, built-in friends, someone who could empathize with you when you had a problem. We didn't need a psychiatrist when we felt overwhelmed. We just walked across the street and had someone who listened. Most of the time your own problems seemed small compared to theirs. We wondered how Dorothy down the street managed with six small children. "Oh, walk by her house. She just keeps the radio on so loud she can't hear them," was the explanation given.

We had coffee together, exchanged recipes, and on weekends the men were out mowing the lawn or the kids were playing ball in the street with daddy. That was life in the suburbs in the late '50s and early '60s. Like the TV shows, Ozzie and Harriet and Leave it to Beaver. Ostensibly, that is.

One never knows what is going on behind closed doors. Inside my house I was trying to deal with an alcoholic husband, trying to protect my children from that fact. When my neighbor was over for morning coffee, I didn't want to answer the phone because I knew it could be someone asking why we hadn't paid a bill. As the children grew older, they became the victims of his drunken behavior when he staggered in and yelled at them, and the most embarrassing time for them was when he turned a corner too sharply and smashed into a neighbor's garage. The car was chained to a post for several days so the damage could be assessed. My daughter's friends asked, "Isn't that your Dad's car?" How does a child handle such painfully embarrassing events? How did it affect their lives? I ask.

There were too many of these humiliating experiences. I should have gotten out of the marriage earlier, but that wouldn't have been easy at that time. It was only when I was making enough money to support myself and my family, and when there was no hope of saving the marriage that I got a divorce. Fortunately, it was an amicable one.

Before he began drinking too much Jack was a good father. He was a cub master, took the kids to the zoo, the park, to Chicago to visit all the places kids should see, including Marshall Fields at Christmas. He could be verbally abusive, but never struck me or the children. He did smash a fresh blueberry pie on the floor one time when he got angry and shoved me out of the way. After his binges, he was always sorry. He had a lot of good qualities: He was intelligent, charming, empathetic, sensitive, and always a good lover.

Unfortunately, my children also have some of his bad genes: the tendency toward alcoholism. My son was an alcoholic and had been living with his alcoholic father in Florida, who had given up on him after numerous legal and financial problems. He moved to Texas, but continued to drink and mess up his life: arrested for possession of cocaine, auto accidents, broken bones, and finally a felony charge. He had reached bottom, and had no one to turn to now except his mother. Donald and I told him he could come to Arizona only under the condition that he enter a treatment facility first. He had no options at this time and was in rehab in Sedona for six weeks, and sober for 10 years.

During those years he was a delight to have around, was helpful, and got along very well with Donald. Then a number of things went wrong in his life: He lost his job, his girlfriend kicked him out, and a product he had invested in was taken off the market by the government. (It was a drug detection kit for parents, one that was being used then and now by law enforcement agencies. It is now available to parents.) Despite his felony charge he was able to buy a gun and one night he got drunk and used it on himself. He had been told by several who knew him well that he could be bi-polar and should see a doctor. I saw those highs and lows myself and felt helpless, especially when he talked about suicide. I offered to pay for the doctor's visit and told him to call the Suicide Hot Line if he ever felt that desperate. The one thing I couldn't do was pick up a 47-year-old man like a baby and haul him off to the doctor. He always had some excuse "I will when I have time." "I will when I have the money." "It's nothing I can't handle."

Anyone who has lost a child will tell you that it is a devastating experience, one that takes a long time to even talk about. My oldest daughter worries me because she often drinks too much, but she has an enabling husband so there is little that we can do. My other two daughters and I have tried an intervention, but it failed. They are aware of the genetic makeup and are afraid that drinking could lead to problems for them. Nan, who never displayed any alcohol-related behavior problems as far as I could see, decided to join AA. She prefers not to take any chances.

In my younger days, I had times when I had too much to drink, but for most of my life, I look at a glass of wine as something that goes with a nice dinner, or a beer, a thirst quencher on a hot day. And a good martini with good friends can't be beat. But I don't have those genes that tell me I need a drink, or that I should get drunk.

There are merits to both alcohol and chocolate, but overindulgence has a price. I believe in moderation. If you can't stay away from gambling, then you have a problem, but an occasional trip to Vegas can be fun. The casinos are worth seeing. If you've never been to Venice, a much cleaner version can be seen at the Venetian. The hand-blown glass ceiling by David Chihuly at the Bellagio is spectacular. Vegas never got much of our money although Don and I were there dozens of times, often combining a bridge tournament with a little vacation.

You don't win money at duplicate bridge, just master points, points that can't even be traded in for mileage, cash, or some premium you don't need. It's all fun for me and the best part is that it gets me out of the house. There are goals to be achieved, and most of us who start playing the game hope to become a Life Master. The American Contract Bridge League has done a fantastic job of holding that master point carrot out in front of the players. After I became a Life Master I lost interest in achieving any other goal, realizing if you play well, and a lot, and go to tournaments, you will naturally advance to another level. However, becoming a gold or diamond life master is an incentive for many, and gives the professional player the status he needs to charge a lot of money for his services. Some nationally-known pros get more than $1,000 dollars a day for tournament play. At the local level there are many who make a little money by charging a player anywhere from

$25.00 to more than $150.00 for an afternoon game that lasts about three hours.

Bridge is a challenging game. I am glad I learned it when I was a young. The game can be played in its simplest form, by standards established and made popular by Eli Culbertson in the '30s, and later improved by Charles Goren's point count system. Now you and your partner can play a system that is very different, and add gadgets that help you bid better so that you can arrive at the best contract. The bidding has become more scientific. A lot of the guesswork has been removed.

My creative nature found a new outlet when my husband asked me to write a system that resembled what the experts were playing. In standard bridge a club is a club; in their system, a club simply said you had 16 or 17 points. From the 250 pages Don received from a friend who had been on the U.S. bridge team I created a new system for my husband and me that was about 15 pages long, and now is played by several others.

Because the game has added so much joy to my life for over 60 years, I think it's only right to give something back to the game. I have been a publicity chairman, newsletter editor, served on unit boards, and I currently write a "Faces Behind the Cards" column for our local newsletter. It has been proven that the game can stimulate the mind's thought processes and help deter dementia and Alzheimers. Those bridge connections in my husband's brain had been so solidly entrenched that although he had lost his ability to read or add or think logically, he was able to play bridge until the end. Much of it was rote, but he was still good enough so that we rarely came in below average. And once, about a month before he died, we came in first, and everyone cheered.

Chapter 14

Age is Just an Attitude

Seventy and eighty are just numbers. We shouldn't fear them any more than we did when we were approaching 30, or OMG, I'm going to be 50, or 60! We made it, didn't we? A few bumps and bruises along the way, but I think this trip is a great experience and I just want to keep on going.

Harvey Mackay, the popular columnist and writer of business books, has this advice, "Act the age you want to be, not the age others expect."

Aging brings challenges and losses. When my vision was failing, cataract surgery miraculously corrected my sight. When I couldn't hear well, I got hearing aids. When some of my teeth had to be extracted, I invested in implants. When my arthritic hip made it difficult to walk and affected my quality of life, I had surgery. The artificial hip has served me well, although it's always annoying to have to go through a body scan when I go through airport security. I am most grateful for modern medicine—and the fact that I can afford to invest in dental implants and hearing aids. Medicare does not cover those items.

Nicholas Wade, in his book, *Your Body Is Younger Than You Think*, tells how most of the body's tissues are in constant renewal and how most molecules in a cell are constantly replaced but DNA is not, backing up his information with scientific studies. The bottom line is: whatever our age, our body is many years younger. My question is: If the body is so perpetually youthful and vigorous and so capable of renewing its tissues, why doesn't the regeneration continue forever?

I don't mean to sound like an arrogant know-it-all. I don't like that Dee. I just feel very fortunate that I grew up in a loving family and learned a lot during my 83 years of living. I want to share some of my ideas for looking good and being happy as an octogenarian who is living alone. Your ideas may be a lot better than mine. And you may not be enjoying good health, so some of my ideas may not be within your realm of possibility. I understand that, and I hope you will understand my thoughts are just that: my thoughts.

We know our past shapes *who* we are and we can learn about our medical history by looking at our genealogy. Thanks to good genes, I am healthy, active and loving life at my age. Grateful to my ancestors, I don't take their gift for granted. I do try to live a healthy lifestyle.

Our grandparents, even our parents, weren't aware of the link between health and lifestyle. It's different today. Over the past 100 years we've seen the development of vaccines, better sanitation, and public health messages have awakened us to the dangers of smoking and obesity. We know we should get flu and pneumonia shots, buckle up, drive sober, drink moderately, keep our blood pressure under control, and use our medications and prescription drugs wisely.

As a young mother I never thought about exercise, but I skied and swam, took care of four kids, and cooked and cleaned. So that counts as exercise during those years, right? I took a yoga class once and that was in the days when there was only one kind of yoga: hatha, where you did asanas (postures) and repeated a mantra while in a lotus position –which I have never been able to do. After I retired I decided that it was time to take care of myself. I changed my eating habits and began to exercise over 25 years ago. I still maintain those disciplined habits, slipping now and then, but getting back to them shortly.

My diet is a healthy one. Breakfast usually consists of a bowl of cereal (usually oatmeal, grape nuts or a fiber cereal) with fruit and skim milk. At 10 a.m. I'll have a piece of fruit or a slice of whole wheat or nine-grain toast with peanut butter or hummus. Lunch is half a tuna, egg salad, chicken, turkey, or salmon sandwich, usually a leftover from dinner the night before. I make sure I have a few ounces of protein so I won't get hungry during the afternoon. Dinner is a glass of wine while grilling or poaching my fish or chicken and fixing a salad. I might add some couscous, rice, pasta or half a sweet potato. I don't eat pork or beef unless I am invited to someone's house and they are serving it. I often stop at a restaurant for dinner after playing bridge. The portions are usually too large so I'll have enough for dinner the next day.

I grew up in a Scandinavian home where the meal and the white plate were hard to tell apart. White bread, white potatoes, creamed peas... ah, there's a piece of beef! Cooked till gray. Actually, my mother was considered a good cook. In those days we didn't think of eliminating fats and sugar from our diet. My dad would sop up the bacon grease with his toast and we always had sweets in the house. No one in my family was overweight. We all worked hard and walked more. Today I avoid the white foods, fats and sugar. I keep my meat or fish portion the size of a deck of cards. A bridge or poker deck, not a Canasta deck! I do watch the scales and cut back if I have over-indulged and added pounds.

As we get older we lose flexibility and my arthritis tells me that it's time to move those joints. A lot of thought has to be put into getting my stiffened joints up and out of the seat after a three-hour movie. I usually exercise five or six times a week for a minimum of 30 minutes. Now it is such a habit I have guilt feelings when I skip a day. I count running around doing errands and shopping, often using a pedometer to see how far I've walked. I'm always surprised when I check it and see I have covered over four miles on a shopping trip. But I'm not a shopper so my exercise is dedicated to many other activities. My favorite is water aerobics. I put on my headphones and an hour goes by so fast. The neighbors probably wonder what that crazy lady in the pool is listening to every Sunday morning at 10 o'clock. There I am, laughing out loud during Prairie Home Companion, listening to Garrison Keillor talk about Lake Wobegon, *where the women are strong, the men, good looking, and all the children, above average.*

I also make sure I lift weights and do stretching exercises a couple times a week. I do most of my walking on the treadmill because it is safer and more productive. I go at a steady pace and I hold on so I won't fall. The Fear of Falling is always there. I have been careless on a couple occasions and fallen, dislocated my shoulder and sprained my thumb. I hear this scenario too often: He or she fell, broke a hip, went to the hospital, got pneumonia, and died.

I try to stay focused. I know what I need to do for my body. I stretch and take deep breaths. I often do isometric exercises while at the computer or on the phone. If I'm vacuuming, I do lunges across the room. Just keep moving, I tell myself. I like to have music on while working around the house. Sometimes I just can't help but cha,cha,cha or boogie to the tune. There are great exercise tapes and DVDs, which are good motivators. Besides, it's nice not to have to get dressed to go to the gym. I occasionally play my Pilates tape, but the pool, whether aerobic exercises or swimming, is heavenly and so easy on the joints.

Yoga classes have grown in popularity. However, yoga today isn't the yoga of 40 years ago. It may be combined with Pilates, other exercises, and sometimes done in an overly hot room. So ask what is expected of you if you plan to enroll. They'll tell you "go at your own pace," but you may not want to be in a class with agile 30-year-olds who pop up effortlessly from a prone to upright position without using their hands. That, on the other hand, isn't quite as intimidating as their bodies and sexy workout garb. If you're one of those who becomes motivated only when others are working out around you, then it's a good idea to join a health club or the local Y.

I have no credentials for my diet or exercise program. I just happen to look good and feel great for my age. The surgeon who did my hip replacement thought he'd have to do the other one in a few years. That was ten years ago! I just keep exercising, and that left hip tells me when I need to rest. You're getting my opinions because this is *my* book. It works for me. The things I'm talking about can be found in many magazines or books.

How often do you walk into a room for something . . . and then forget what you were after? Join the club. I've done that for years, and it isn't necessarily a sign of dementia or Alzheimers—just too much in our computer brain. Researchers are constantly discovering new ways to help us enjoy good health as we get older. Getting older doesn't doom us to poor health. Physical exercise helps our brain by providing it with sufficient oxygen, but it's a good idea to actually have exercises for the brain. Playing bridge and other mental exercises, such as working crossword puzzles, reading, writing, playing board or card games, or participating in group discussions have been proven to deter the onset of dementia.

When you are alone, no husband, no children in the house, it's time to enjoy that freedom and become a bit hedonistic. It is a time to love who we are, a time to put ourselves first, but realizing that what we do for others often brings the most joy. If we don't love ourselves when we are alone, we end up feeling sorry for ourselves, often bitter, complaining, and sad. That attitude perpetuates loneliness because who wants that kind of person around? Extending kindness to others usually diminishes our own problems, increases our self-worth, makes us the kind of person people like to be with. Buddhism has enlightened the world for centuries:

You yourself, as much as anybody, deserves your love and affection.

A lot of things can give us pleasure. It might be taking a class in painting or photography. Travel. A book club. Or a garden club. One of my friends had always wanted to play the piano, so when he retired he rented a piano and took lessons. I am forever curious, and surprised what will pique my interest, expand my circle of friends, and add happiness to my life. The computer can be as frustrating as it is exciting. I'm a dummy when it comes to computers, but I had to learn how to use it if I wanted to write a book. I did it. I'm getting better at it all the time; now I'd give up my microwave oven before my computer. It is a wonderful way to stay in touch with friends and family. Much more effective and satisfying than playing telephone tag with the answering machine. I am on Facebook and twitter, even though I really don't know what I'm doing most of the time.

"Frankly, Facebook seems like a big waste of time," quipped 88-year-old Betty White in her monologue on Saturday Night Live. Millions of Facebook members wanted the actress—so well-known for her role in the "Golden Girls" TV show—to host SNL, and that episode received the highest ratings in years. It turned out to be an effective use of time for the twitters and tweeters and profitable for NBC. To me, it's just fun.

Volunteerism offers us a chance to meet and socialize with other people, maybe some who are younger. And that's good! I find that if I socialize only with people my age the conversation too often is centered on health problems, or who died, or who is having trouble with their kids. Or, even worse, how brilliant their kids and grandkids are! Some of my dearest friends are in their 40s and 50s and when we get together it's like college days. We talk about poetry, history, religion, politics, books. I leave their house, feeling younger, stimulated, and ready to order a book from Amazon.

I don't think "growing old gracefully" means living in a velour warmup suit and having gray hair. Nor does it mean wearing what a teen-aged granddaughter would wear and dying your hair coal black. Friends wondered if the 75-year-old bridge player was getting senile when she walked into a room wearing cut-offs and heels. "My 12-year granddaughter has those shorts," someone said.

It seems as if dress codes have collapsed almost everywhere, but I don't want to join the crowd of slobs that parade around with food stains on their clothes, breasts drooping to the waist (no worry there!), or a big belly flowing over it. I know, *comfort first*. I don't want to look as if I don't care for myself. I don't want to look as if I'm ready to be shipped off to a nursing home.

You and I can, of course, have any color hair we want, but when the wrinkles appear, a solid black certainly accentuates them. Belts may be "in" but if the waistline isn't what it used to be—and whose is?—then it's a fashion to forgo. The loose tops that gently cover the middle are usually the most flattering. I wouldn't go out in this Arizona sun without sun screen and I am in and out of the pool before 11 a.m. Makeup is where I am susceptible to all the promises made, and I give them a try if they aren't in the ridiculously high-priced range. I have settled on some favorites: good old Ponds, the product my mother always used, Maybelline mascara, and Revlon lipstick. They're cheap, compared to a lot of products on the market, and seem to work well.

A few weeks ago I was walking through the cosmetics department of Saks and noticed Swiss products advertised. I remembered I needed moisturizer and stopped and asked the salesgirl what they had. She brought out a small jar which she thought would be good for my complexion and I asked her how much it was. She calmly said, "One thousand dollars." I couldn't contain my reaction; I gasped, and instinctively exploded into laughter that could be heard throughout the store. I stopped at Walmart on the way home and picked up Ponds.

Face lifts scare me. But then I was so chicken about having my ears pierced I had to wait until my stepdaughter gave me the piercing as a gift for my 50th birthday. I had wanted pierced ears for years because my lobes are small; I was constantly losing one of my clip-on earrings. I had been in line on two occasions to have it done, but changed my mind before it was my turn. The day Fran came to pick me up for the "ear surgery" I had a double scotch first. And Fran was right, it didn't hurt. I didn't feel a thing. I may have staggered a bit when I walked.

There are good face lifts and bad face lifts and too many face lifts. I hate that mouth that reaches from ear-to-ear. It was probably Phyllis Diller who said, "Some women have had so many lifts they have to wear a turtle neck so their navel won't show." Nips and tucks seem to work just fine for many, and it is amazing how some injections can help erase wrinkles and sagging faces and how lasers can remove the sun spots. If it makes you feel better about yourself and if you can afford it, go for it.

It's worth it to do what you should do to try and stay healthy. There is still so much to do, so much to see, and so much to learn. I am doing my best to prolong that final trip. Why not? I'm enjoying life and have no proof that anything else is better. I quote Richard Dawkins in his brilliant book on evolution, *The Ancestors Tale*:

> *Not only is life on this planet amazing, and deeply satisfying, to all whose senses have not become dulled by familiarity: the very fact that we have evolved the brain power to understand our evolutionary genes redoubles the amazement and compounds the satisfaction. My objection to supernatural beliefs is precisely that they miserably fail to do justice to the sublime grandeur of the real world.*

I ask myself, how could anything be any better for that poor and naïve farmer's daughter who was able to work her way through college, become a reporter and editor, and a very independent woman with a wonderful family? I know the love and freedom my family gave me and the hardships I faced—and those Scandinavian genes—have been critical in my evolution. My life's financial problems, disappointments, failures, illness, suicide, and death challenged my character. They imbued me with empathy, sympathy, and a better understanding of other's problems. My past has helped me deal with problems rationally and sensibly, thus avoiding major damage to my mind and body. If I feel down and wonder *why does this happen to me?* it doesn't take much talking or reading to find out that my problems are miniscule compared to someone else's.

When I didn't know how to deal with my alcoholic husband I found help in AlAnon. When I found it hard to understand my second husband's crazy behavior, I turned to Alzheimer's support groups. Work, hobbies, support groups, and simply taking care of yourself go a long way toward enjoying this wonderful life on earth.

You're pissed at someone? Get over it, forgive them. Make like a tough Bronx New Yorker and *Fugged-i-bowd-it*. The "revenge is sweet" idea is usually an ephemeral victory with a long-term destruction to relationships. Albert Schweitzer compared revenge to a rolling stone that is forced up the hill, "only to return with greater violence." Charlotte Bronte likened revenge to an aromatic wine on swallowing it, warm and dry, but its after-flavor— "as if I had been poisoned." Martin Luther King said, "An eye for an eye leaves everyone blind." The Talmuds's advice: "Live well. It is the greatest revenge." A willingness to forgive and forget makes us the superior one, not the victim. Vengeful actions and negative attitudes are stressful and toxic to the body. They are just another contributing factor to those wrinkles we try to avoid—wrinkles that are more than skin-deep, ones that can't be erased by a $1,000-dollar jar of moisturizer, I'm sure.

I was lucky, as a reporter you can't be a perfectionist. You have deadlines, consequently your best effort within that time frame has to be good enough. I don't recall who said perfectionism is *subjective, ridiculous and neurotic,* but it is so true. What's perfect to someone else may not be perfect to you. It's impossible to do a great job with your marriage, your home, your kids, your career, your body, friendships and health. My daughter had to call me after she had taken her five-year-old to see Santa and he asked Emily if she had been a good girl. "Good enough," she said. *Just like her grandma!*

I take vitamins and a prescription drug for lowering my cholesterol, which seems to be a problem that runs in my family, and not related to my diet. I know that I have to treat my mind and body well in order to enjoy and participate in the activities that are part of my life.

Just because we now may be without a partner doesn't mean we should give up sex. A lot of women I know say they just aren't interested in sex any more. But, good luck, if you think you can find someone who just wants to take you out to dinner or the theater. The male animal doesn't give up his sexual desires easily and Viagra is always there to help.

Although most women's sexual interests decline after 70, I admit I miss that intimacy. Even a sneezing fit that takes over my body like a tsunami can't beat a good orgasm. When a comedienne was asked about her sex life, she responded, "It's great, I just wish I had a partner." Vibrators can be ordered over the internet and they arrive in a plain brown wrapper.

According to various sources on aging, having sex can increase longevity. It releases hormones in the body, increases intimacy and bonding, and works against loneliness and depression. As natural lubrication decreases when we age, this is easily resolved with lubricants. And there is no reason to feel guilty about masturbation.

Although I have many interests to keep me busy, I cherish my aloneness, my quiet times. I'm comfortable with who I am. I am amused as I realize that so many things I thought I knew when I was young are wrong.

Sixty years ago, I knew everything; now, I know nothing: education is a progressive discovery of our own ignorance.

Will Durant, American historian (1885-1981)

I don't in any way have all the answers now, but *that* is not important to me. Our time on earth is limited, so it makes good sense to live life to the fullest, embracing knowledge and new experiences. God, our soul and spirit, angels and infinity are far easier to accept than to explain. What I do know is this: It is good to be alive.

Carl and Carrie Olson History

Olaf Peterson (1823-1913) and Maria Persdotter (1822-1913) were born in Varmland, Sweden, and married in 1845. They came to the United States in 1881 and settled in Sargent,ND.

Olaf and Maria's children, all born in Sweden, were: Carl Olson (1854-1940), Andrew Olson (1860-1947), Carrie (Mrs. Gust Nordin (1857-1936), Henry Walstead (1864-1932) and Alfred Olson.

Carl Olson came to the United States in 1879 and married Carrie Lofven (Loven), who was born in 1864 to Jon Persson Lofven (born in 1829) and Anna Oldsdotter (1828-1900), both of Solberg, Eksharad, Sweden. Carrie came here from Sweden in 1886 and was married to Carl that year in Willmar, Minnesota. Carrie died in 1934. (Carrie's sister, Anna, born in 1869, married Carl's brother, Andrew Olson, in 1889. She died in 1956.)

Carl and Carrie Olson's 12 Children:
(1854-1940) (1864-1934)

Carl William (1888-1969)   Algot (1889-1974)

Henry Hjalmer (1890-1949)   Milton Fredrick (1891-1918,flu pandemic)

Ethel Elvira Woldman (1892-1939)   Elmer Gerhard (1893-1992)

Walter C. (1895-?)   Esther Elizabeth Swedberg (1900-1979)

Twins: Stanley Leonard and Cecil Benhard (1902-1975)

Twins: Parker Engel and Parnell Elvin (1912-1979)

The Eight Cousins

Cecil Olson married Esther Pederson and they had two children, **Dolores (Dee),** born in 1926, and **LeRoy,** born in 1931. Dolores married Jack Liebeler and had four children and was divorced and married Donald Horwitz. She has six grandchildren. Dee's address: 15225 N.100th St. Unit 1212, Scottsdale, AZ 85260. LeRoy, a retired postal employee, married Lolly Peterson and they have two daughters,four grandchildren and one great-grandchild. An avid fisherman and hunter, Lee has been forced to limit those activities because of emphysema. He and his wife live at 1413 18th St. SW, Willmar, MN 56201.

Stanley Olson and his wife Bergliot had one daughter, **Evonne,** who was born in 1939. Evonne was married to Russell Grunseth, and they had three sons and a daughter. Russell died in an auto accident in 1977; she married Wyman Frost in 1989. Her hobbies are sewing, quilting and reading and she enjoys cooking and baking. She has ten grandchildren and seven great-grandchildren. They live on a seven-acre farm: 8085 150St. SE, Sacred Heart, Minnesota 56285

Elmer Olson married Rena Johnson and had one daughter, **Shirley (Lu),** an artist, who was born in 1927. She and her husband, Harvey Wilson, spent most of their life in Hawaii, retiring to Whidbey Island, and later to 23825 S. Stoney Lake Dr., Sun Lakes, AZ 85248. They have two sons and four grandchildren. Despite many physical problems, they lead an active social life, and travel to Hawaii and Whidbey to visit friends and relatives.

Esther Olson married Axel Swedberg when she was 38 and had two children, **Richard,** born in 1939, and **Eunice,** 1943. Richard, an attorney, and his wife, Blanche, have two grown children. They live at 815 Locust Rd., Wilmette, Il 60091. Richard is an attorney in Wilmette, Illinois. He and his wife, a retired flight attendant, have two children and three grandchildren. They have a cottage on Washington Island, near Green Bay. Blanche has multiple sclerosis and recently underwent surgery for lung cancer

Eunice is married to Thomas Shoaff, an attorney, and they live at 2130 Forest Park Blvd., Fort Wayne, IN 46805. Eunice and Tom have three grown sons. They spend time there and at a cottage in northern Michigan "where they kayak and hike and take Mr. Finnegan, their

Portuguese water dog." They have three grown sons. Eunice calls herself "a Pilates junkie," and likes to cook, bake bread, and garden.

Parnell Olson married Gertrude Bendler, and they had two children, **Bob** and **Karen**. Gertrude was the last surviving member of the second generation of Olsons, dying in 2009 at the age of 98. Bob was born in 1945 and is an attorney. He and his wife, Mary Ann, live at 924 S. Western IL 60068, and they have two children.

Karen Bendler, born in 1941, took her mother's surname after she was divorced. She is an attorney, serving as a magistrate in the Alaska court system. She has two children. Karen's address after she retires at the end of August, 2010, will be 1101 Cordova Square #111, Anchorage, AK 99501.

Acknowledgments

M y memories alone would not have been enough for this book. I owe my deepest thanks to my cousin Evonne Frost, who provided me with important documents and obitiuaries. Thanks Evonne for keeping such good records.

Four cousins whom I met over the internet for the first time -- Richard Swedberg, Eunice Shoaff, Bob Olson and Karen Bendler -- were most helpful in relaying stories and providing photographs. My cousin Lu Wilson was, as usual, terrific, reminiscing with me about our times on the farm, and the many other times we were together, and offering her creative ideas. My brother, LeRoy Olson, added humorous anecdotes and made sure I had my facts right by questioning some of my stories. During the course of researching the book I consulted a great number of books and articles, as well as the internet, to verify or add information.

My daughters Nancy Sloan-Okey and JoAnne Liebeler suggested several changes that clarified and improved the text. I am deeply grateful to Edward Bronstien for his advice, inspiration and continued interest in the story of my life. I ultimately decided on listing only four generations of Olsons in the history, I sincerely want to thank Alec Olson for checking out the family genealogy for me.

My deepest gratitude and special thanks goes to Joyce Goff, who was a critical reader and gave me exactly the right kind of advice. It took her objective and intelligent look at the manuscript that resulted in a book that includes a family history *and* my life experiences—a book that I hope will bring back memories and provide some joy and inspiration to those who read it.

Awards and Recognition

Community Leader Award: Minneapolis YWCA, 1981
First Prize: Pre-retirement video tape for Honeywell, National Industrial Film Festival, 1981
Gold Award: Total Communications Project, National United Way, Honeywell, 1980
Gold Award for Excellence in Graphics. Honeywell, National United Way, 1977
First Prize, Editor & Publisher magazine, youth series, *The South Bend Tribune*, 1971
HEW Award: nursing home series, *The South Bend Tribune*, 1970

Author of *Modern Math* magazine (*The South Bend Tribune*), a primer for parents, 1966; used by Office of Economic Opportunity in Head Start programs.
Co-author (with Edward Bronstien), *Who Made My Bed*, 2010

"Over the years you have shouldered an enormous amount of work without complaint. . .the number of well chosen, thoughtfully arranged paragraphs that have come from you are beyond counting. You've battled hard to break down our male chauvinistic attitudes, and rightly so."
Dean Randall, Honeywell vice president, communications.

"… I have heard many favorable comments on the article you wrote about energy stored in outer space. . .they came from both scientists and non-scientists." *Dr. Milton Burton, director of Radiation Laboratory, University of Notre Dame.*

". . .Your account of the student protest over Cambodia and Father Hesburgh's statements was well written and objective . . . and was placed in the Congressional Record (May 7, 1970)." *John Brademas, Indiana, U.S. House of Representatives.*

"Many thanks for your help on that inflation speech. It went over very well." *Edson W. Spencer, Honeywell president, 1974.*

"As always, Dee, you do a complete, professional super job." *J. W. Read, Honeywell manager, communications.*